Drighlington Reflections and Reminiscences

The West Riding keeps one eye on the mills and markets and the other on the moors.

JB Priestley, *English Journey*, 1934

Drighlington Reflections and Reminiscences

Drighlington Parish Council

Compiled by Parish Councillors
Janet Scholes, Arthur Thornton
and Steven Slater

Published in 2009 by Drighlington Parish Council

British Library Cataloguing in Publication Data:
a catalogue record for this book is available from
the British Library.

ISBN-13: 978-0-9563832-0-4

Printed and bound in Great Britain by
Delta Design and Print, Morley, Leeds

Map of Drighlington 1882–1892 reproduced with the permission of the
Ordnance Survey
Thanks to Edward Rushworth for the image of the Booth Bros
letterhead (www.rushworth.com)

Thanks to Stephen White for the aerial
view of Drighlington

Cover design by Stuart Wheatman

Contents

Introduction

The aim of this book is to capture the personal memories and reminiscences of some of the older residents of Drighlington, depicting a way of life very different from the one we live today, and to safeguard those memories for future generations before they become lost forever.

By reading these stories you will see that life was by no means easy for 'ordinary folk', and perhaps your life and life in the village will take on a different perspective.

Our thanks to Brian Furniss, Drighlington's local historian, for sharing his archives and for allowing us to use some of his vast collection of photographs. Thanks also to Jill Morris, the director of Morley Literature Festival, for her help with all things practical.

Finally, a special thanks to those members of the community who generously gave their time and permission to be interviewed and their memories recorded. It has been an honour and a privilege to work with them. We hope you enjoy your trip down memory lane.

Janet Scholes
Steven Slater
Arthur Thornton
October 2009

Mary Blockley
1931–

I was born in April 1931. My earliest memories: I was born at Dean Park Farm near the Egg Packers. My dad used to milk cows and we had a milk round; the horse was called Darkie and everybody knew him. We used to go morning and tea time to Hammond Crescent, Beechwood Avenue, Wood View Grove ... All over the village I used to go with Dad on the float. I have a sister who is three years younger than me. Our house had two bedrooms, a bathroom, kitchen, living room and a dairy attached at the end. Our toilet was outside and we had an ash pit. Men used to come with a horse and cart to empty it. I went to Drighlington School. I didn't like school so much; I used to love to get home. I wasn't born a good scholar. It was alright, though, we had some nice teachers and friends.

My mother used to help in the dairy but then she started to be poorly, then my dad had to finish farming in 1945. We had a farm sale and he kept the milk round on and bought milk from the dairy, and then we went to Moorland House on Moorland Road to look after Grandma Bower. Their house was like a castle to look at. She died in 1948, then we came to live where I live now. Grandma Bower had lived at Dean Farm, the place where I was born. Her parents were Martha and Joe Dean; the farm was named after them. I don't know what they did, it was before my time.

I went to work in a place at Bradford doing office work. I didn't go there by choice, but if I hadn't I would have had to go into the mill. My sister went to Morley Grammar School but I didn't. She became a teacher. We didn't have holidays, too busy working on the farm, but I did go to Isle of Wight with the vicar of St Paul's and his daughter: it was like going abroad.

We used to do all the mowing with horses; tractors hadn't come in. We had three shire horses, one called Duke, Darkie, can't remember the other one.

I met my husband at Doncaster Market. We used to go there to buy calves. He came from Flanshaw in Wakefield. We both worked down on the farm after we were married. We used to go to Otley to buy cattle. My husband's father had a coal round; he had a cattle wagon, took the body off and used it for delivering coal. We never had a honeymoon and went straight back to work on the farm. We lived where I live now – nearly sixty years in all. We lived in a house down the lane for three years before building this one. Wilf Grayshon built this bungalow in 1951 and my mum died before it was done, so she never moved in. In our spare time we went to the Young Farmers' Club and to different people's farms and agricultural shows.

We always had plenty of milk and grew turnips and potatoes and bought the rest of our food as normal. I remember when we lived at Dean Farm it belonged to the Lord of the Manor, somebody called Day, and I used to go to the Malt Shovel to pay rent once a year. There were a lot of properties belonging to the Lord of the Manor, including John Thornton's nursery.

Zion chapel, Wakefield Road

There were a lot more shops, a bread shop, paper shop; we used to go to Mrs Bastow's to get our Christmas toys and sweets. She lived on Bradford

Road. Where the Co-op is now it used to be a draper's, butcher's, grocery, with a slaughterhouse round the back, and the village was almost self-sufficient. King Street had a bank, Post Office, paper shop, draper's, chemist and bakery, the Lion Store on Three Lane Ends and Zion church round the corner. There was a butcher near the brickworks.

Characters I remember were an old chap who lived down Spring Gardens called Johnny Butterfield, who looked like a tramp, and across the road from Day's pet shop in a little cottage a chap lived there who we called 'Doubtful', I don't know why. My sister and I used to go to another little cottage where three old ladies lived. They used to look after us, and we took puppies in our dolls' prams.

I wouldn't want to change anything I've done in my life; I love farming and looking after cattle (I'm getting a bit too old now). They're in the field at the back of my house, just eight store cattle, and I buy them at twelve months old and keep them for a summer and a winter. After two years I sell on, but I never go to market, I don't like it. They stay out all the time and I feed them on a morning. I just shout and they come to me. It keeps me fit and young, but it's bad in winter as the field gets very wet.

I remember having a radio and had to get batteries from Cyril Walker; he'd charge them up and bring them round to your house. He lived at Nethertown at the top of Old Lane. I remember Peter Kemp and his brother David; their father Joe Kemp founded the Egg Packers. I remember Mr and Mrs Rushforth who had the brickworks. We had four children who are all farmers, David, Elizabeth, Sally and Rosemary, but they do other things as well.

A lot of people I knew have died and new people live here now that I don't know.

Mervyn Crabtree
1938–

I was born in Morley Hall in August 1938; our home was at Moor Top. That particular house is still standing but a lot of the houses around ours have been knocked down. It was a one up and one down with an outside toilet, and that was a bit of an experience. You went down a couple of steps and there was a wooden seat with a hole in the middle, you know what I mean, with a nail and squares of newspaper, and it was definitely not for the faint hearted, especially in winter, but it was alright when my mother put warm ash in from the fire. We all used to fight like mad to be first in. It was a dry ash pit, you know. There used to be a couple of men with a horse and cart that used to come with shovels and empty the toilet.

We had a tin bath and it hung on the cellar door. We used to have a Yorkshire range, which my mother used to black lead, and it shone like coal when she'd done it. My sister, who was older than me, told me that when my mother was having me in Morley Hall my father was looking after her and he decided that they'd have a fry up for tea. Well, he put a pan on the range and it was cast iron, and left it to do some washing up. He went back to the pan to put the one and only egg in for my sister, and she said when the egg hit the pan there was such a crack and it disappeared up the chimney. My dad went outside to see if it was on the roof, but he never saw it again.

Moor Top

Then when I was a young kid I was friendly with Billy Varley, who lived next door, about the same age as me. One day the pair of us decided we'd go look for coal, and we went and dug a hole on the moor. We got two shovels and we worked all day and dug well. It got to tea time and we were both jiggered. We'd only knocked off for our dinner. So we went home for tea. Well, our neighbours were called Fanny and Dossie Lockwood, and they had two kids, but Fanny was a right funny 'un, you never used to see her out during the day. But after dark she used to walk round the moor.

Well, this particular evening she decided to walk across the moor, and guess what she fell into: this hole me and Billy'd dug, and she couldn't get out. Anyway, she started shouting for help but nobody heard her for ages. My dad went to the toilet and heard her shouting; he had to pull her out of this hole. Well, me and Billy had to put up with a lot of stick after that; the woman was never quite the same with us, but you couldn't blame her.

The other thing that sticks in my mind was Farmer Moxon; he had the farm by the side of St Paul's church. There used to be a manor house on the farm but it's all pulled down now, but there are some outbuildings left just as you turn on to Back Lane. They were part of Moxon's farm. He used to run his cows on the moor and just let them roam. In fact there was an incident when the farmer got gored by his bull; he had it on a chain, it got wrapped round his legs and pulled him down. Anyway, I digress. One day my mother was looking out of the window across the moor when she noticed a cow on the moor eating the washing on the line. She rushed out and got a prop and chased the cow off, but she had to wash a bodice again as it was all green and slimy.

St Paul's church, Whitehall Road

Next door but one was a family called Pinfield; they had three kids and the youngest one was Colin. At that time he was about three years old. On this particular day it had been raining all morning and when the rain stopped Billy and I went to Mrs Pinfield's and asked to take Colin out in his pushchair. She said, 'OK, but be careful and don't go so far,' so we took Colin out. Well! We came across a huge puddle. We were running along pushing Colin, and this puddle looked lovely. Well, we ran through in our wellies and pushing the pushchair and Colin was screaming and laughing. We got to the other side of the puddle and turned round to go back through. As it turned out, there was a pot hole in the middle of this puddle that we had managed to miss on the first run through. Well, the wheels of the pushchair went into this pothole that we couldn't see and Colin, who wasn't strapped in, did the most beautiful dive for a three year old you have ever seen. He got up covered from head to foot in mud; we took him home screaming his head off and looking like a drowned rat and ran to our homes. When we got home we remembered we'd left the pushchair in the middle of the puddle. Well, Mrs Pinfield came to our house and didn't half play hell with my mother. I couldn't sit down for a week after that. Well, I didn't know there was a pot hole, did I! Another time I went with two older boys to the mill dam. It was surrounded by a wall and fence and we all climbed over the wall. We were looking for newts and frogspawn. The water was fairly well down at that time. There we were, fishing for newts, and I thought somebody nudged me but nobody owned up at the time, and I fell into the water. Well, I can remember going down twice, going down, then coming up for air, then going down again, then one of the older boys grabbed my collar and hauled me on to the bank, soaking wet and coughing up half the dam. I was bawling my head off. The two older boys scooted off and left me to make my own way home, wet through, squelching all the way. When I got home my mother had gone down to Aunt Florrie's and my dad was at work, so the house was locked, so I squelched all the way to Aunt Florrie's, who lived in a house where the Trawler fish shop is now. When I got there my mother played merry hell with me, took all my clothes off and dried me down and dressed me in a pair of our June's knickers. Well, I was more upset being dressed in the knickers than falling in the dam; I was mortified, especially when Auntie's three daughters came in.

I remember my father being friendly with Mr and Mrs Clegg; they lived in a bungalow on Moorside Road. Mr Clegg was part of the family that owned the new textile mill. One day my parents went over for a meal and Mr Clegg was telling my father about the clock on the mantelpiece that'd been 'nowt but trouble': 'We've 'ad it to a clock mender an' 'e's 'ad a go at it but it still won't keep going.'

So, Dad said he would have a look at it, but he was no clock mender. So they wrapped this clock up in brown paper and then he took the clock home. At that time the living room was lit with an old gas mantle, which you had to light with a match; well, my dad put the clock on the table, which was under the mantle, and climbed on to it to turn on the gas and light the mantle. When he was getting down he nudged the clock and it fell on the floor, which was made of Yorkstone flags, no carpets like we have today. Well, there were cogs, wheels and springs rolling about the floor from this clock. We gathered all the pieces, springs, cogs, screws, the lot, together and put them on the table. My dad was mortified what Mr Clegg would say when he saw the pile of remains.

Anyway, my dad set to in his spare time and put the clock back together again. It took a long time but he managed it, but he had one cog left and there was no place it could go. He looked and looked and couldn't find where it went, but the funny thing is, the clock worked. My dad kept the clock for a further three weeks and it held its time and never stopped, so he took it back to Mr Clegg and never mentioned to him about the spare cog. Anyway, about five or six weeks passed; he saw Mr Clegg and asked ''Ow's the clock?'

And he said, 'Great, still working,' and he'd only wound it up once in all that time. As far as we know it never lost as much as a second.

We had a radio, the old valve type, and it was well before television. Me and my sister used to cut up old clothing for my mother to make list rugs to cover the flagged floor, and we would have a new list rug made each Easter. That was how a lot of children spent their evenings. Some people used to call them peggy rugs.

Barron's mill

My mother was a weaver at Barron's mill, which is now the lighting company [Southgate Lighting Ltd]. It used to be a three-storey mill at one time. My father worked at Farnell's; now, Farnell's was a saw mill and then it changed to Holdsworth's wire works, so my dad became a wire drawer. It's all houses now, Newcastle Close, I believe. In the wire drawing they used to use a lot of acid and I remember they had to take a lot of the soil away before they built the houses because it was contaminated. I can remember Dad's overalls; they always had little holes where they'd been splashed with the stuff. This acid must have been lethal stuff and when you think on there was no safety gear in those days. All my dad had was a pair of overalls and a pair of gloves. Anyway, I was growing up and there were four of us in this one up one down, so my mother put her name down for a council house and we eventually got one in Oakwell Close, so we moved into this council house that the builders had just finished. It was like a palace, three bedrooms inside, a kitchen complete with a gas cooker with a Belfast sink and next to that we had a galvanised gas clothes boiler. It was very modern, fitted cupboards in the kitchen and electric lights. We didn't have a fridge; we had a pantry with a cold slab to put food on. They were still building the houses when we moved in.

Barron's mill in recent years

Three of us were playing football after school one day when one of us kicked the ball up on to the roof, and it lodged in the gutter, so I said I could shin up the drainpipe and get it. They were cast iron pipes in those days. Anyway, I shinned up the fall pipe, got on the gutter and was edging along the slates to get to the ball when my mother walked round the corner out of the ginnel. She was going to a whist drive that she liked. I froze, thinking she wouldn't spot me, but she did, so I had to get down the fall pipe pretty quick. And I didn't get my ball. My mother never got to the whist drive that night because she marched me back home and it was early to bed for me.

Drighlington and Adwalton rugby club

We used to walk to school in those days, and we used a path behind Lambert's bakery. They used to call him Teacake Ted. It's where the rugby club is now. The path was called the Bawk. I don't know why it was called that but it was. I was at Drighlington School until I was thirteen and sat for a place at grammar school, the old 11 Plus, but I failed that. But then I got the chance to go to technical college at Batley, or the one at Dewsbury. I sat both those exams and passed both, but chose Batley. I used to get a bus to the Spread Eagle pub and then get one to Batley. The Spread Eagle was where the roundabout is now. Opposite the pub used to be a fish shop owned by a Jewish couple, and she was a big, big woman. One particular day the fish shop was full and she was chatting away, ladling the fish out, and her false teeth came out and fell in the fryer. When she turned round the shop was empty. She lost a lot of customers that day.

When I left school I got a job as an apprentice joiner working for Harry Naylor's at Bruntcliffe. The apprenticeship ran from fifteen years of age to twenty-one and my wages were two pounds and ten shillings a week. I used to travel by bike to work. Harry Naylor's workshop was two floors and upstairs he had his work benches. Underneath there was a garage and Harry's office and on the other side a small machine shop. In there were three machines, all worked off one electric motor. There were leather belts and gears connecting all the machines together. These belts ran under the floor and up to the machines, which was fine in most cases, but if you got wet weather for a spell these leather belts would tighten and when you started the motor running there would be an almighty crack and the belts would come off. The office Harry had was Dickensian, and you've never seen one like it in your life. The window looked down to the yard gates. There was a high desk with one high stool and his filing system was two hooks. When the bills came in they were put on one hook and when they were paid he would take them off and put them on the other one. He had a ledger on the desk, but that was his way.

Harry didn't used to say anything if you were five minutes late going home, but if you were five minutes early there would be hell on. Those were the days, eh! One time there were four lads, all about eighteen years old, and we decided to save our money and have a week's holiday at the Isle of Man. That was a big deal in those days. We got a train from Drighlington to Liverpool and then the ferry. We had a rare old time. We got this boarding house with four big bedrooms. Two rooms were set aside for us and the other two for a group of girls, and the landlady was a right puritan. She made it quite clear that there would be no fraternising (you know what I mean); even when you went to the toilet she knew 'cos the landing had a creaky floor, and she'd actually come up to see where you were and that you went straight back to the room. Anyroad, I remember one day it was pouring with rain and she'd gone shopping. We had a right old time, but it never happened again. On the way back from our jollies we got on the train at Liverpool to come back, and when we were on the train the guard told us it wasn't stopping at Drighlington. We were a bit miffed as we'd have to go to Bradford and then come back by bus. Well, when the train got near to Drighlington (it used to run where the bypass is now) it went really slow, so we decided to get off. We lowered the window and threw our cases out, and then we jumped, but as we jumped the guard was looking out of his window and he went past us shaking his fist and shouting. But we couldn't hear what he said because of the noise and off he went into the distance. We walked home across Penfields. It was better than catching a bus from Bradford, 'cos after a week in the Isle of Man we'd had enough.

Well, that's the most amusing memories I can remember, but when I'd done my national service I noticed a big difference in Drighlington. There used to be such a lot of industry in Drig, and now all that's gone. There was something like five textile mills: Appleyard's by the brickworks, there was one where the lighting company is now, opposite the football pitches, the New Mill, there was one down at Cockersdale, and I think that that's still standing. They didn't just give work to the people in the village; people came from all over the surrounding area to work in Drighlington. There used to be a soap works and they used to make massive bars for the mills, who would cut them to small pieces for the wash basins to cut down on pilfering. There was the Salvation Army in what's now the Atlas engineering works. If you look on the building there's a round circle with Salvation Army carved into it. I got a cornet loaned by the band, but the neighbours complained about the noise I made practising, so I had to give it up.

A few years ago we used to get a piper practising on the moor every week. He'd march up and down playing the bagpipes for about an hour, but then all of a sudden he stopped coming. I remember people going to Cockersdale for the day; when I was little there was a lake and people used to picnic and go for boat rides in their blazers and straw hats, and they used to have garden parties. Charlie Smith's parents used to live in that cottage down there and they had the boat at the side of the cottage. The skip man, BW Skips, he has the cottage now, and the lake was at the side, but it's not there now.

You know, years ago there was everything you needed in Drighlington and the surrounding area; you didn't have to leave the village because you could get everything you wanted from the shops, but most of them have gone now. Yes, it was a very self-contained area.

I remember the farmer called Brennan whose farm used to be behind the White Hart pub where the bottle banks are now, and his fields were where Walton Drive is now, and that area. They were all rhubarb fields. Well, he barricaded himself in his farmhouse with his shotgun for some reason. I can't remember the incident that caused him to do it, but it must've been serious: I don't think it was because we used to help ourselves to his rhubarb, that's for sure!

The Websters used to grow forced rhubarb, and I remember as a kid going into the sheds, which were lit just by candles, and you could hear the rhubarb growing it used to grow so quickly, trying to reach the light. You could hear it crackling. It grew about three to four inches in a day. You can tell if the rhubarb's forced 'cos it's right thin. They still grow it the same way nowadays. Moorhouse's jam factory at Beeston used to take all the rhubarb they could lay their hands on for the jams. Happy days.

The Spread Eagle, Gildersome crossroads

Viva Harding
1922–

Eighty-six years I've lived in Drighlington. I was the first child to be born in Fairfax Avenue, when it was only that part just round the green. Then when I was seven the bottom part of Fairfax Avenue was built, then, of course, the top part, Oakwell, was built, and that was after the war. I lived with my granny and then my mother and father got a house in Hammond Crescent when I was nine, but I still lived with my granny until I was fourteen because my mother worked, and of course then when I left school I went to the Egg Station to work as a packer. The Egg Station was opened on 1 October 1934, my birthday. I went to live at home as my mother gave up working. I was a packer, and then I became a candler, testing the eggs for quality. Then I got married, and when I was having my first child I had to leave work because there was such a lot of heavy lifting. So I became a housewife. I lived with my parents, and when my first child was born my husband was stationed down at Newquay in Cornwall, and I went down to him and took Gerald, my son, and we were there until he got moved to Exeter, but there was no place for me to go so I came home again. When Gerald was two we got a little house, which isn't there now, up Whitehall Road, by the fish shop – the Dolphin. John was born in 1946, and George came out of the Air Force 'cos he had been a regular; his time was up. He went to work at the wire works and didn't like it; it wasn't what he was used to. He'd been his own boss in the Air Force and he now had to do as he was told.

Fairfax Avenue

We then got a flat in Gildersome. Gerald was ten and John was seven. But it was one of those family flats and ooh, and the noise – it nearly drove you crackers! There were two bedrooms, a living room, a bathroom and a kitchen and they were in blocks of four. But with families they were noisy and we could listen to everything that was going on upstairs. But Ivan, the man upstairs, didn't believe us – he pooh-poohed the idea. I just said, 'Well, when your telly's on, if it's the same programme as we've got on, we just watch the picture and listen to yours. And when your father comes we can listen to the conversation.' His father had a very loud voice. And I said, 'Will you please buy a new bed!' It was very embarrassing, listening to the 'performance' – it was the legs, the bedstead.

Then he came down one day and said, 'I've come to apologise.'

I said, 'What for?'

'You said you could hear everything. Well, we've had something wrong with our fireplace and had to take the fireplace and the hearth out, and between our floor and your ceiling it's hollow. That's why you're hearing everything.'

It was getting to me; I had a nervous breakdown. We used to talk in whispers, and slippers were always by the back door so we could slip them on. We daren't shout at the kids. It was really uncomfortable. Then we had a chance of a swap, to go into Oakwell Road – right at the very top, the last house – the midwife lived there with her mother, who was elderly, and she wanted something easier, so we did a swap. But oh, what a mucky house when we moved in! We had a living kitchen, a sitting room, two bedrooms and a bathroom. It was a lovely house though, and we lived there for forty years. We were very happy, but both George and I started to be poorly. He had a three-way bypass, a pacemaker and a burst ulcer all in six months. He was never any good after that; he used to just sit – he couldn't do anything for himself and so we applied for a bungalow or a flat. We moved in the March into the flat and George lived here just eighteen months, and then had to go into Siegen Manor because I couldn't cope. He was there just short of six months. Then they took him to Seacroft: he was there for six weeks and then he died.

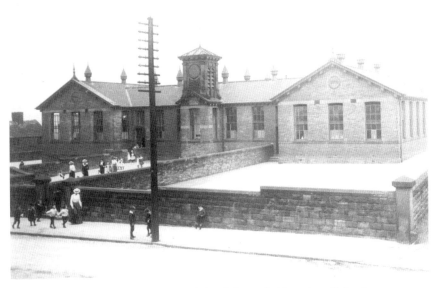

Drighlington Board School, formerly Margetson School

I went to Atherton's College of Knowledge, which is what they used to call the school on Whitehall Road. Atherton was slang – the slang name for Adwalton. Adwalton finishes at the Post Office and then it's Drighlington. I enjoyed my school days and I can remember every teacher by name. I can see them now, and remember that later one of my teachers had a serious illness and they told her to change her job. She was very good at baking and decorating cakes so she got that little shop on Bradford Road that used to be the flower shop. I was working at the Egg Station at the time so I used to take liquid eggs and cracked eggs for her bakery. When George and I got married she made us our wedding cake. It was illegal to have icing on your cake during the war – but I had it! I had a lovely square two-tier cake, beautifully iced, with a silver vase on the top with pink roses, and that was our wedding present from 'Auntie Bea'. She became our boys' godmother in time. Then she started catering and I used to work with her. I used to work in the bakehouse. We loved Auntie Bea – Beatrice Forbes – who unfortunately didn't have any children. She used to make crinoline ladies from icing and won lots of prizes. She made beautiful cakes.

There was no such thing as a school uniform unless you went to the grammar school; in those days it didn't matter so long as you were tidily dressed. There were some very poor children went to Drighlington School, but I was fortunate because my granny could sew and my auntie, who lived with us, was a hand sewer and she used to make me beautiful clothes. My dad's sister was a tailoress so I was always well dressed. Happy memories!

When I was a teenager my mother always wanted me to be well dressed and when Matthias Robinson's was on the go I always used to go for my velour school hat, which cost twelve shillings and eleven pence, which was a lot of money, but they had to last two years.

George and I were pen friends for three and a half years. My cousin, Alan, was in Iraq with George and Alan wrote to me and asked if I'd like to write to this young airman who'd no one to write to except his parents. Owt for a lark, I was only sixteen. So I said yes, and George sent me a letter and a photograph and I thought, 'Ooh, a bit of alright!' That was in July 1939, and we got married in June 1942 and we had almost fifty-eight years together.

I used to go to the Fellowship of Marriage, which was a younger branch of the Mothers' Union, and we were made members on 3 June 1943. Mrs Silk was our enrolling officer. We worked for the church; any money we made was for the church. In 1960 we stopped working for the church when a new scheme came in 'cos they didn't need the money, so we started working for Macmillan nurses. We did all sorts of things to make money, and we could make money! Jack Sanderson, the councillor, used to call us the fountain of money because whatever we did we made money on it. We bought some lovely things for the church: the big beech hedge round the commemorative garden, altar frontals, kneelers, curtains, bibles: you name it we bought it. We used to get Steradent tubes and fill them with the old-fashioned thrupenny bits with the sides on. The tubes used to hold ten shillings. The members kept dwindling and dwindling, they were all dying off, and I'm the only member left of the Mothers' Union and the Fellowship of Marriage.

Drighlington was a proper village. I was never here at Whitsuntide 'cos I always used to go to see my grandparents at Ripon, but the week after, which was Trinity weekend, there was Atherton Feast, which used to come on the Thursday to the fairground at the bottom of the Waltons and on Friday night it was free rides to make sure everything was safe. Weeks before the Feast my granny would start and do all the pickles and suchlike and she had a new peggy rug on a frame: we always used to have a new hearth rug for feast weekend. She'd do the pickles and we always saved a Christmas cake and on the Friday she would get a big piece of beef, which would be roasting all day, and she would make a big bowl of ginger wine and after lunch on the Saturday everything was cleared away and the dining room table would be set, best table cloth, best tea service all came out, and all the cakes and everything. The meat would come out and be sliced, all the pickles put in fancy dishes, and all the relations would start coming and we'd have a knife-and-fork tea. After tea we all went down to the fairground and us kids would only have about sixpence and we'd have to make it last as long as we could. Our first job was to buy a poke of either coconut strands dipped in sugar, which was a penny, or a poke of broken brandy snap and then we'd wander round and have ride or two, which cost a penny a go, but we always saved one to have a penny worth of chips from Miss Johnson's fish shop, now a Chinese. We had a really wonderful day.

Everybody came back then and had sandwiches and of course on the Sunday there used to be a band on the cricket field by the fairground and a Mrs Pergota and her daughter had a stall in the fairground and sold sweets near the bottom of the cricket field. There used to be a big square of canvas and you used to have to throw coppers in to pay to go in, but we always bought a bit of something at Mrs Pergota's. We all used to walk round and round the field showing off our Whitsuntide clothes. On the Monday there was a big cricket match and that meant the feast was over and done with. In midsummer was the carnival – the children chose who had to be queen and the retinue. Whoever wanted to be queen from the top class had to put their name down and the other pupils voted for who they wanted to be queen. The girls in the next class down had to put their names forward to be maids of honour and they were voted for. Of course, there were the page boys who had to be voted for as well, but they were separate from the girls in those days. It was mixed classes in the infants to start with, then the girls and boys became separated. Then came the thrill of getting measured, choosing the material, and the girls, mothers, aunts and grandmas would be busy with the sewing machines. It would be fever pitch, and it was a carnival – a real procession.

The week before, about eight married ladies used to dress up as gypsies and they borrowed a barrel organ from somewhere – but no monkey – and they would go into a different part of Drighlington and Adwalton every night of that week collecting money. The carnival would start with the procession, which started from a different part of the village in different years. The retiring queen would be dressed in white with a royal blue cape and the new queen would be in white with a red velvet cape. There were no motors then, so we had coal carts and suchlike. Mr Millicent-Brook, who lived on Bradford Road, had a big open stable and they used to bring a cart there all cleaned up and polished. Butter used to come in barrels then and the Co-op used to save the hoops from the barrels and we used to trim them with crepe paper and make roses and fasten them on, and the cart all trimmed up used to look like a flower garden. There was one cart for the new queen and one for the retiring queen and the attendants were on the carts with them. A brass band from Gomersal would lead the procession and then there was a comic band and people all dressed up in fancy dress; children were in fancy dress, with decorated prams and decorated bicycles, and different organisations and the Sunday schools had a cart with the children on, all trimmed up. There would be a big stage in the field at the crossroads and the queens and dignitaries of the village would be there. The dignitaries would do a bit of spouting and the new queen would be crowned. Then they would come off the stage and the new queen would walk all the way round the cricket field showing off her clothes. Then there was the judging of the best bike and best pram. The cricket club was only a wooden hut in those days and all the prizes would be kept in there – they called it the tea tent. After the queen had done her walkabout there would be races for the children. There were no refreshments like there are now: it used to be ice cream, and if Mr Burnley had time from Gildersome he would come, so we could have different ice cream sellers and it was beautiful. It was all over and done with by about seven. In King Street on the pavement there would be little stalls from the crossroads up with people selling things and all the houses had bunting across the street. We really did look forward to carnival time.

The White Hart pub, Three Lane Ends

The Trawler fish shop was a house, next door was the Co-op boot and shoe shop; they sold shoes at the bottom and had a tailor's department upstairs. Then the shop on the corner was a jeweller. It was still Co-op property and then it became the Co-op greengrocery. Next to where the barber's is was the Co-op butcher, then the grocer and then the draper. Next to the Atlas engineering works was Harry Smith's the confectioner's – he sold beautiful boiled ham; all the food was made on the premises. There was also a butcher's shop on the land in front of the scout hut. Opposite the school was Miss Burnett's sweet shop and there was Totham's sweet shop next to it and on the other side of the road just below the school there was a sugar boiling place that belonged to Totham's. During the war if you took two pounds of sugar and a shilling you could have two pounds of hard-boiled sweets, which made your rations go further. There was a fish shop and the old Co-op at Cockersdale, where Hirst Amusements is now, and a shop which sold everything. In King Street there was Scott's Pop and next door to what was the bank was a fish shop owned by Little Mother Redman.

She had a seat and a little table inside so you could eat your fish and chips inside – she was a funny little woman. That became Miss Walker's wool and baby shop, next door to the Post Office, and next door was a paper shop – a little wooden hut owned by Aveyard – and then the Black Bull. Moorside builders was a barber's, Calvert's, and a bit further up was Broscombe's shop and yard who sold all manner of things; you could even buy wedding presents there. The Village Pantry used to be a butcher's, which belonged to some German people. Mr and Mrs Minz and their Ada came from Germany after the First World War. He was real old fashioned with a long curly moustache. They were a lovely couple who made beautiful food, penny ducks with veils on – faggots made in a big tray with skin on the top, and the skin was called the veil. When my granny used to send me for some she always used to say 'Think on and bring some with veils on' but I don't know why. Kitson's drapery stood where Londis is: they were very old fashioned, vests and knickers hung up on coathangers – it was laughable to go in. Then there was Thomson's chemist shop, just a poky little affair, then where Rushforth's is was Timmy Mason's, which was taken over by Scanlon's, a shop and warehouse. A bit further up was Robertshaw and Melton's. Then you get to Three Lane Ends. There was the Lion Store, and when it opened if you spent five shillings you got a shopping basket. Going round the bend you came to Lambert's bakery, and at the bottom of Fairfax was Mitchell's shop. She was a bit of a greengrocer but on a Friday night she used to boil ham shanks and make mushy peas and we'd go down with a jug and sixpence for a jug full of peas. Next door was Gettings; he sold sweets and bread. On the other side of the road opposite at the corner was Butcher Brown's and then a row of cottages which became BRK and the 4711 – is that cologne? I have some in the bathroom – I mean 7-11, and then the Wagon and Horses, and further down the White Hart and at Three Lane Ends it was the Unicorn. It had been a pub in olden days but then it was a fish shop – Fatty Akroyd had that – and then at the other side was a little bakery and sweet shop and she used to make beautiful sponge buns with real fresh cream, which were three pence. If my granny could afford it when I was going back to school after lunch she used to say, 'Call at Miss Hanson's and order two cream buns for three pence,' and then I'd call and pick them up after school. We used to cut them into two so that two buns would do four of us; me and granny would have one and my auntie and my mother the other. We'd no money, so things had to go a long way.

The Unicorn, Wakefield Road

Everybody used to put a little bit by all year for special occasions, like Christmas. My granny was a very good cook and she would get a sheep's head for three pence and she'd stand it in salt water all night and clean it. Next morning she'd take its eyes out and boil it and then scrape all the meat out back into the stock and add vegetables and it was a pan of good broth. That day we'd have dumplings with it and the following day what was left we'd have with Yorkshire puddings, and we always had a sweet, either bread pudding or rice pudding or something like. She'd seven grandchildren to feed at lunchtime because our mothers worked, but we never went hungry. Another day she'd get some tripe and onions and potatoes and a vegetable and we always had something varied. She could make anything. I got so as I could make a dinner out of a dishcloth, because during the war we had to.

My mother worked at the mill [now Southgate Lighting] and my father worked at Hudson's foundry. Before the war there was only work two days one week and three days another – there was no dole – so that's why Mam had to go out to work. She was a weaver. It was only when the war started my dad got full-time work. My grandfather came from Ripon and he brought all his family to work at Hudson's foundry before the First World War and he became one of the bosses, and during the war the women of the family went to work there. My dad started out as an apprentice floor moulder –

they made the turntables for the trains and train wheels, and the bogies for the mines.

The houses at Fairfax where I lived as a child were expensive houses. They were fourteen shillings and sixpence per week rent, which was half a week's wage in those days. The headmaster and headmistress and the borough surveyor lived there. The houses were built round the green, and as children if we were playing with a ball and the ball went on to the grass you daren't get it – you'd to go and ask Mr Harrop or Miss Phillips if you could get your ball, or else you were in trouble. Those days we were brought up with respect.

One day a man would come selling cold fried fish and another day one would come round selling crumpets. There used to be a couple who would come round from Birkenshaw and we called them 'the OK Couple' because she was K legged and he was bow legged. They had a big barrel cart and when you opened the door there were all shelves inside. They sold buttons and wool and stuff like that. On a Saturday afternoon there used to be a fella come with a horse and cart and his cart had all little doors on everything that was inside – compact, it was, only the buckets and brushes would be swinging underneath. He sold vinegar and all sorts of household things. In summertime the ice cream man would come round on an evening 'cos he had a milk round during the day; in winter time they used to come round with pies and peas. You had no need to go out of the village because they came to you and there were so many shops and businesses. The only thing you needed to go out of the village for was furniture. You went to the Co-op and got a chitty and you went to Leeds Co-op to choose what you wanted, but paid for it at Drighlington Co-op. If you wanted anything special in clothing you would go to the Co-op and get a chitty and go to Leeds Co-op or to Goodson's, which was on Boar Lane: a very high-class couturier.

The Egg Station in a previous life was the picture house. They had evening shows and it was four pence on the front seats and then six pence as you went up. The balcony was nine pence. There was a shop called Dibney's near the pictures where we used to go for our sweets before the show and they had little dishes with fancy doilies full of sweets in the window. At the bottom of Station Road and Moorland Road there used to be Walker's shop. Mrs Walker made nice bread. She had a seat inside the shop and you could have a buttered teacake and a pot of tea if you wanted. Then there was Sherwin's fish shop, and he used to go for his fish with a white enamel bucket. All the mills were working and the workers used to go there for their fish and chips.

We used to play skipping, hoops, whip and top and hopscotch and relivo, kick the can and piggy stick – a bit of wood with a pointed end, and you hit it and when it jumped up you hit it again and you had to stride to where it landed, and the one that went the most strides was the winner. Relivo was like hide and seek. We always had something to do and we used to love baking day – if Granny or one of the neighbours made oven bottom or flat cakes we had them with margarine and treacle whilst they were warm. It was gorgeous. We had some very happy times as children and it cost nothing.

I had a holiday every year and went to Blackpool. I hate Blackpool, but Granny's sister had a boarding house in Charnley Road and so Granny wanted to see her sister every year. We couldn't afford for Dad to go with us – he used to go to his mother's at Ripon. Cyril Walker used to take us in his big old-fashioned taxi. There'd be my mother, my granny, two aunties, one uncle, two cousins and me. Granny had a big tin trunk and for weeks she would save tinned stuff in the trunk with her clothes. The Thursday before the carter would come and collect the trunk, which went by rail so that when we got there the trunk was already there. All we had were our cases fastened on the back of the taxi. We'd take sandwiches with us and when we got to Gisburn there was a really big green house where we got a cup of tea and used the loo so the engine could cool. We went to the theatre every night and when we arrived we went round all the theatres and booked for the first turn every night. In the morning we'd go on the beach and play and in the afternoon the parents wanted to rest, so us kids would go round Olympia and Hills bazaar. We'd no money to spend, but we used to look. After tea we'd go to the theatre and on the way back it was a penn'orth of chips for our supper. At my auntie's you kept yourself. You all had your own cupboard to put your tinned stuff in. When we got back from the theatre there would be a dinner plate with a slice of bacon, tomato and an egg for each person, and your name would be written on a piece of greaseproof. Breakfast. We had our own tea, we bought our own meat, all fresh because there were no fridges, and vegetables, apart from potatoes, which my auntie supplied but we paid for. Auntie would cook the meal while we were on the beach and she would provide the sweet – rice pudding or blackberry tart. But we didn't like Aunt Minnie. She believed children should be seen but not heard. At tea time we'd have tinned salmon, and fruit and cream for afters. We used to call at a bakery and we could choose a cake each and I always wanted an elephant's foot. We used to go for a week at a time. Cyril would take us one week and bring someone else the next before taking us back. If we hadn't used Cyril's taxi we would have had to go by train to Blackpool Central Station. The third week in August was Morley Feast week and Drighlington holidays. We'd no money, but we made our own amusement.

On Saturday night we'd go into Bradford or Leeds, when stuff was cheapest, with a plaited straw bag. If we went to Bradford we'd do a bit of shopping as the shops were open until nine, and we'd call at Pie Toms where my mum and dad could have a plate of pie and mushy peas for three pence, and my plate of peas cost one penny. It was a luxury, because we didn't have enough money to do it every week. If Dad and I went to Leeds we always made a beeline for the fish stall: three oysters, and he'd have two and I'd have one. They were three for sixpence. If we went to St George's Hall with Granny, Mum and Granny would go downstairs, where it was a shilling each, and upstairs it was nine pence for me and Dad. That was a treat. Before the buses we used to go on the trams from the crossroads, and that cost four pence to go to Bradford. We used to sit on the end at the back, 'cos if you did that you got a longer ride. Happy days.

Booth Bros, now Southgate Lighting, Moorland Road

Winnie Brook
1917–

I was born on 20 November 1917. I'm only 91! My earliest childhood memories ... I used to run around a lot and be very active; I used to be taken down in the woods a lot by my dad, which we knew as Sykes Wood. I remember starting school at Drighlington and used to walk it. The infant teachers were Miss Bentham and Miss Fairburn. They both lived in Drighlington. One classroom had a fireplace in it with a fireguard round. I can remember it now. We used to come home for dinner. Our house just had a living room, cellar, two bedrooms and toilet outside. There were a lot of steps outside: we lived down the 'branch' down from Valley Inn. I loved my time down Cockersdale. I had a really happy childhood. My dad worked at Mark Darnbrough's opposite Valley Inn, as a brass moulder. My granddad worked there; he was also a brass moulder. My mother never worked. Our social life was spent at Nethertown chapel. I went to Sunday school for seven years without a break and got a medal. When we went on holiday we had to go to Sunday school. Sunday morning we got dressed up to go, and when we came home we got changed. After dinner we got dressed up again and went back to chapel and did the same at night. Afterwards we had a little walk. I was always in trouble for kicking my shoe toes and playing with my hat. Sundays were very boring and you couldn't play with a ball or anything. Our Sunday reading was the children's Sunday newspaper.

Berry Gardens, behind the Valley pub

Mondays were best. We had a little fish shop on Whitehall Road and we could have a penn'orth of chips. It was our highlight. We had Berry Gardens down Cockersdale, and they had a boat, a fairly big boat. It was a halfpenny for children to go on and a penny for adults. It didn't go very far. There were swings and at night they put some wood down and had dancing. I was a little wood nymph really, 'cos I was always there. There was a waterfall and the best water I ever had, really cold.

Berry Gardens

A girl once said to me they had 'monkey on t' tap', and I went to her house and thought I was going to see a real monkey, but it was a block of wood on the tap as they hadn't paid their water rates. There was a ghost on Drighlington moor at Christmas. When I was fourteen on Christmas Eve we sang carols at people's houses and we found out the 'ghost' was a man running round with a sheet over his head. We played whip and top and with a wood ring we hit with a stick and with skipping ropes. An indoor game was housey housey; I used to hate that! I used to cheat and was put to bed. I played dominoes.

There was a little brown bus that went to Morley, but we didn't have any buses at Cockersdale: we had to walk to Farnley Moor Top to get the bus to Leeds. My granddad lived with us, he was a sweet old man, and used to go to Leeds market on a Tuesday. He had a great big handkerchief and went to market and got a rabbit and tied it in the handkerchief on a stick, and they used to call him Dick Whittington. To go to Gildersome we had to walk up New Lane or across fields. We used to go sledging: we walked up that big hill and sledged down, and you came home with your clothes wet through. I had a lovely time.

My dad always saw we went away for a week. We got two pence spending money and spent one penny and saved the other for a holiday. We went to Blackpool one year, then Scarborough or Bridlington the other. My dad didn't get paid for holidays. We went into lodging houses, not in hotels. We went on a Saturday and had to wait 'til Monday to get acclimatised before we could go into the sea. We had to come to Drighlington station for a train, so my dad's friend Johnny Gilson, who had a horse and cart, he took us to the station.

I was fourteen when we moved up to Drighlington. We went into Hammond Crescent when the houses were new. We had our own council in Drig. Clifford Sutcliffe was on the council and he got us this council house; he was gas manager at the gas works. It had an indoor toilet and bathroom: it was marvellous. There was a gas works at Cockersdale and during one night the gasometer was rising and we all had to go into the woods as we thought it was going to burst. It didn't, but we thought it was great. A man lived by us; he worked at the gas works. He always slept on an afternoon with a tea cosy on his head.

I met my other half (Stead) at Nethertown chapel. His mother and father were caretakers there. There were tennis courts there then, it was lovely.

Houses are built round there now. I went to work in tailoring in Leeds. Stead was a driver. I used to start at eight o'clock and go on the half past seven bus for two shillings and sixpence a week. I finished at five o'clock and Stead worked until seven o'clock.

We had no money for a honeymoon. I'm still waiting! Our first home together was in Hammond Crescent. My dad was allowed to go to the Valley pub on a Friday night and my sister Joyce and I had a bath then. It was a tin bath kept down in the cellar, and we got bathed in front of an open fire. When I was married we did a lot of walking down Tong on a Sunday night. We walked to Pudsey just to go to the park and when I had children I walked there in school holidays and took sandwiches and pop.

The thing I would have changed would have been to go back to Cockersdale, but I wouldn't change my life. I had a happy life, lovely parents, and Saturday morning I came to shop at Drighlington and my grandma made a Yorkshire pudding to eat on my way back home. I used to get in trouble a lot: I wasn't naughty, just mischievous. I never had any illness, whooping cough or anything. I once borrowed a penny from a teacher to get home on the bus and got into trouble. When I asked my granddad if I could borrow a penny he'd say 'When you borrow, always pay back!' Two old ladies lived near us and I went to the shop for one, and she gave me a penny. My mother made me give it back 'cos I had to do it without being paid. I worked twenty-two years at Drighlington School, and I was 'temporary' all the time. I loved my time at the school. One little boy had a lovely round face. I could have taken him home, and he wanted to come and live with me. He presented me with my radio when I left. I got on with all the teachers: Miss Bottomly, Miss Smith, who came on a motorbike and used to put children over her knee and slap their bottoms when they were naughty. We had some nice Christmas dinners.

I consider I am one of the luckiest people living. Five years ago I had cancer and apart from poor eyesight I consider myself lucky. I have a lovely family. I wasn't a goody goody. I had one sister who I lost at forty-three. I regretted going to live in Drighlington at fourteen; it was awful coming to live in an estate and I couldn't understand my mother coming to live there. I cried my eyes out. It was free and easy down at Cockersdale. I wish I had taken more notice at school. I learnt the piano; George Gomersal taught me. Cockersdale was my life. Once, two weeks before Christmas, we went to see Santa in Leeds and had tea in a cafe. It was lovely and a highlight of my life.

Cockersdale woods

Queen Elizabeth II visiting King Street, Drighlington, 1954

Stanley Jackson
1929–

My grandfather was president of the Veterans' Association, which had its meetings in Drighlington park. Henry White was my grandfather's name and his wife was related to the Boddys who emigrated to America. Anne Boddy married a man called Skillington and his daughter married my grandfather. The veterans' hut started about 1934 and was somewhere behind where the swings are now. Up to two or three years ago the club still met.

I was born in King Street, where Londis is now: in fact I was probably born where the checkout is now. I was three months old when we moved to Fairfax Avenue and I lived there up to getting married. In those days King Street looked a lot different, in fact, the Londis store that's there now was a herbalist before being taken over as a chemist. Later on the chemist moved to Whitehall Road. The house on Fairfax was a corporation house.

I had an older sister and two younger sisters. The houses in Fairfax had flush toilets whereas most houses in Drighlington didn't; you had to go down the yard. There was one place down Back Lane which still had a midden.

When we were children we had the Whit walk, when all the churches gathered together and walked from one end of the village to the other and finished up in a field somewhere. There would be organised games and that was always an exciting time. There would be a piano on the back of a horse and cart so we could sing.

When I was four or five I first went to school. I remember one day (we used to go home for lunch at that time, and from Fairfax Avenue to the school was quite a walk) I was supposed to wait for my sister, but for some reason I didn't and got to the bottom of Fairfax Avenue to cross the road. I looked both ways very carefully and I was halfway across the road when a car appeared in the distance, and I ran back, and when the car came up to where I was the man got out of the car and crossed me over the road. In those days cars were few and far between; they were nearly always horse-drawn vehicles.

The author, aged five, outside the Fairfax Avenue house

I went from being a good reader to a bad reader because I had a stammer and the teacher, instead of working with me and helping, ridiculed me when I was trying to get words out. Her name was Miss Harper. That was before we went into the big school.

My mum didn't work until war time – she did weaving. Dad worked at the rope and twine works at the end of Tong Lane – Thomas HL Coates – they made string and rope and all this kind of thing. The operative on the main machine when they were making the rope had to walk from one end of the building to the other, which was perhaps a hundred yards, letting out all this rope, so they called that the band walk. During the war Dad went on munitions, to British Beltings at Cleckheaton; they made brake linings (which was an important job), and he also worked weekends – he got time off in lieu but somebody had to be there to activate the air raid warnings and he was the chap that pressed the button that set the alarm off.

Back Lane, opposite St Paul's church

I was fourteen when I left school and went to work at Lloyds Packers, which was in Bradford, and at fourteen I was of course the office junior. I'd been to Fox's School of Commerce and learnt shorthand and typing and book keeping – particularly book keeping. We packed boots for the army and they had about seven million pairs of boots in seven different warehouses dotted around Bradford. Every day we had to give a stock count to the War Department of how many pairs of boots we had. The two lads we had, neither of them were good at arithmetic; one of them, when he couldn't get a balance, used to alter the bottom figure. So when I joined they found out I was good at arithmetic and that quickly became my job, even though the other two lads were more senior than me. In less than twelve months one went into the navy and shortly after the other into the army, so I was 'top dog' then. We also packed all kinds of clothing relief supplies for the refugees. Lloyds was given the job of packing up clothing, dresses, skirts, trousers. These things were made by the clothing manufacturers and supplied to us and I had to do the book keeping for that. The bales went mainly to France and Belgium as the countries were relieved. I worked there for over twenty-three years.

We couldn't afford holidays: we had Bradford holidays, which were the first two weeks in August. I had three aunties and two uncles who lived in Drighlington, and during the second week we used to meet at someone's house one day and we'd go to Birkenshaw park, which was a bigger park than Drighlington with a lot more swings, and another day we'd walk down to Batley park, and that was our holiday. My father had the week off.

I had a gang of pals and five of us went on holiday to Blackpool together when we were about thirteen. At that time things were on ration and so you had to supply your own food. The landlady would cook it. One of the lad's mothers knew the lady we stayed with and she said she would look out for us, and we went three years in succession to Blackpool. We always went on the train and we always had a super time. They charged us thirty shillings. I would say it was unusual at that time for lads of our age to do this. I remember only going to the seaside twice before; then once we went to Scarborough on a trip with all the Sunday schools together. The organisers booked a full train from Drighlington station to Scarborough. I remember I was anxious to get some rock for my mother. I was with my cousin and sister and they were interested in doing what they wanted to do, so when we got to a rock shop I went in and bought my rock. When I came out they'd moved on. I didn't care because I knew exactly where the station was and I made my way there. Of course, they were searching Scarborough high and low to find where I was, and when they did get back to the station there I was safe and sound with the other kids. I really got played pop with for that. The other time was just after the war started – 1939 – I'd be ten, and I went to Blackpool with my grandfather, Henry White, and we had a week's holiday. One day he went to Southport flower show and he was quite keen although he hadn't a garden.

I suppose we didn't think too much about rationing – we'd two ounces of margarine a week, a very small amount of meat, and about one shilling and sixpence in money. The only thing that wasn't on ration was offal and sausage. If you got a joint of meat at the weekend there wasn't much to play with the rest of the week. After the war, two or three years on, some things were still on ration and one of them was bread. In the ration book there was a page for bread units and you took your ration book in and the shopkeeper tore off one little square to say you'd got your ration of bread for that week. One day the policeman called at our house and said, 'Can I speak to Stanley, please?' He knew me because he lived directly across the road from me on Fairfax Avenue, and he says, 'Now Stanley, where were you last night?'

I said, 'I went to the youth group.'

'Are you sure you weren't anywhere near Stevenson's shop?'

'No,' I said.

My mother came in and asked what it was all about, and he explained that the shop had been burgled that night and in the morning, when the police were searching for evidence, there was a page of our bread units on the floor. I told him that I never had them – my mother always had them in her shopping bag, and she must have dropped them during a visit to the shop.

I don't remember going short of anything, but I remember one of my aunties always pestering my mother something terrible because you could only get a small amount of sugar, and my aunties used a lot of sugar. My mother, with four children, was able to keep some aside. Every Christmas they would pester my mother for sugar for the Christmas cake.

Christmases were quite big at one time. We used to go to my auntie's down Back Lane. She lived in the big house, which is still there, and is the oldest house in Drighlington, and we'd go for Christmas dinner and tea. Ours was a big family get-together, probably about fifteen or sixteen of us. We got very little in the way of presents, just a new game, plus an apple, orange and a new penny.

Stevenson's was originally Robertshaw and Melton's; they were old, established Drighlington people and they had a grocery shop in King Street. They sold out to Jesse Stevenson, who was quite a big wholesaler who came from Pudsey. The main shop was the Co-op. There was also a tailor and boot and shoe shop; both belonged to the Co-op. The Co-op had a butcher, a grocer and a draper's. At the corner of the Station Road (now the doctors' car park) there was a little shop which was the Co-op greengrocer's. The Co-op also had a shop at Nethertown. There was another butcher's and grocer's near the Gildersome boundary and at the bottom of Moorside Road there was a butcher's and on the other corner was the Lion Store, a grocery shop which also belonged to the Co-op. People didn't shop in town for the necessities.

The Con Club used to have a bowling green and next door was the police station. The sergeant used to live there and the constable on Fairfax Avenue. There were two cells there.

One of the most regrettable changes is the public transport. When I was a lad you could go to Drighlington station and catch a train to London. I've been told that during the war it was quite possible to leg it off the train at Drig station instead of going into Bradford. My wife travelled to Dewsbury every day on the train to work. There were four buses an hour to Bradford, West Riding. And also from Drig crossroads, Bradford Corporation buses ran every thirty minutes, and four buses an hour went to Leeds. The Morley 'loaf tin', like a minibus, went from the crossroads to Lee Fair, through Morley. During the war when the last bus was at nine, as they had to be back at the depot for ten, the loaf tin came into its own. I've seen as many as fifty people on that bus from Morley Town Hall to Drig. He never left anybody.

They talk about Tingley being the centre of the rhubarb trade these days, but Drighlington must have rivalled it because every farm had a rhubarb shed. There were a lot of farms in Drig: Akroyd's, Stakes', Webster's, Moxon's, Bower's ... probably eight. I used to go pea picking at Farnley. Somebody came to school to ask for volunteers. One or two of my mates went potato picking. Adwalton Cricket Club used to have pigs on the spare ground next to it and behind the doctor's at Three Lane Ends there was a big pig farm.

There used to be a greengrocer called Eastwood who came round with a cart. Another bloke called White, he had a round, and he had a little wooden hut where the bus stop is at the bottom of Oakwell Road, and he sold fish. It said on the back of his cart Bob Green White Grocer or Bob White Green Grocer if you read down or across the panels:

BOB   WHITE
GREEN   GROCER

They were happy although quite isolated days, apart from the Whit walks. We could play out without any fear. When I was about four I had a toy car, as did my mates. Once when it snowed, when I was about three or four, the snow was higher than me. I remember the corporation men shovelling it on to two-wheel carts for tipping on the moor. They must've done this for three days, probably about 1933.

There was an open-cast mine after the war in Akroyd's field.

When the war started they built an air raid shelter behind the school and they asked all the pupils how long it would take them to get home. My mother and father filled in the form and said it would take me twenty minutes, but I was ridiculed for that length of time. Most put ten. They thought it dangerous for all of the children to be in the same place during the war, so they decided to split school between the churches for twelve months or so, so we spent some of our time in the Primitive chapel, which was the Barracuda Youth Club, also Moorside, and the chapel down King Street. We were taken down the woods on a nature study so we wouldn't all be in the same place at the same time if bombs dropped.

Sirens did used to go off, but never during the day. There were one or two incendiary bombs dropped on Moorside Road. There was a high explosive bomb dropped in a field in Tong.

Some shelters were just two pieces of corrugated metal for the sides and panels at the end. Something like six foot square. You had to dig down three or four foot and then erect the shelter with soil. They called them Anderson shelters. There were bigger ones for families, eight or nine foot. The day war was declared Dad went out in the back garden and dug a trench four foot deep ready for the shelter. Everyone was offered one, but if you had a good cellar you didn't need one. My brother-in-law lived in a terrace house in Fagley and the cellar went through the whole of the terrace, so if a house was bombed there was a means of escape through other houses.

We used to go to Morley pictures on a Saturday afternoon, for two pence. It was advertised in the papers that there would be a mock gas raid one Saturday and they let smoke bombs off as we came out of the pictures, and we had to use our gas masks. When we were younger we used to go to Birstall pictures as they cost a penny, and as it was two pence plus bus fare to Morley, it cost five pence all together. It was a penny for hard-boiled sweets; you could get about half a pound, which would last all the time. We used to walk past the fever hospital on the way to Morley, an isolation hospital. We were warned about walking round there. It was used for scarlet fever and smallpox. The young ones were quite often scared.

My favourite film was *Union Pacific* with Randolph Scott. There was always a serial – *Flash Gordon* or the *Lone Ranger* – plus a proper picture.

Trams used to run from Bradford to Drig. If you caught the last tram at nine you caught the last post. There was a post box at the back of the tram where you could post your letter, which would be delivered the next day.

Nights out were usually in Morley and as we got older we went to Bradford.

Sally Dicks' pond! Near the library there used to be houses, six or seven houses, and then a pond with newts and tadpoles. It was great temptation. We'd play football on the moor and walk back past Sally Dicks' pond.

We once got caught pinching strawberries. We took some sugar in a bag and one of the lads was supposed to give us warning, but saw the fella coming and legged it without telling us. We were still in the field when the man came through the fence. We had to apologise and say we wouldn't do it again. Poor fellow used to have all his strawberries pinched. One day we discovered some mushrooms on a muck heap. They were as big as saucers, and we took them home. We'd never had mushrooms before. I was about twelve.

King Street, looking towards the crossroads

King Street Methodist church

Peter Kemp

What became Yorkshire Egg Producers was formed in the early days as an agricultural co-op, in 1934, and based on the site of the old silent picture house on Whitehall Road. It operated up until the war and rationing and then was part of an amalgamation scheme organised by the Ministry of Food. YEP by then was one of the larger operators and it became the co-ordinator of the whole of the North and East Ridings of Yorkshire. It was at the end of the war that YEP was formed – it started life as Poultry Producers WR Ltd. All the small businesses were given the opportunity to amalgamate, which many of them did, and that resulted in 1949 in the formation of YEP, still an agricultural co-op. The building on the opposite side of the road was built in 1948 and 1949 and opened at that time by the Director for Eggs, a man called Jack Peacock, who was with the Ministry. The business progressed over the next several years, developing into Lancashire, Lincolnshire and down into Shropshire, mainly through acquisition of other business and at one time operating fourteen egg packing stations. Changes were then taking place with the development of the battery cage in 1960, and producers were getting considerably larger, but at the end of the 1950s YEP had no less than 15,000 active egg producers from whom they collected each week.

The average collection was at that time two cases of thirty dozen from each of the producers, although as few as one or one and a half dozen came from some of the calls. At that time all of the producers were paid weekly in cash, no cheques, and the cash was delivered the following week by the driver on his way round to pick up the eggs. The changes in the 1960s began and the number of small producers dramatically declined over the next ten to fifteen years, but a few more were added producing free-range eggs, until there were about a hundred farms producing free-range and barn eggs.

Yorkshire Egg Producers

Jim Grayshon
Deceased

At the time of interview, Jim was ninety-five years old and a life-long resident of Drighlington and Adwalton.

I was born in 1882 and went to Drighlington Board School and paid two and a half pence, and I went to half time and went to Tong Lane End, now Lapwater Hall. We started at seven am and finished at twelve there. Back then we had to run to school with a 'time book' and get it signed. At the Board School we paid halfpence for a pot of tea and we had our dinner in the classroom, and then we were ready for the afternoon lessons. I remember my teacher, they called him Sam Abson, he was a very good teacher, but he had some unruly scholars. There were four from Cockersdale. They never came in on time and had the stick twice a day every day because they wouldn't say prayers. They had to go see Mr Higson and hold their hands out and he used to give 'em it. We had to say prayers before we opened the school.

I was a monitor in one of the classes and the teacher was Henry Longbottom. He wasn't so very big, and one of the scholars from Cockersdale, a rubbish lad, George Potts they called him, he'd been doing something and he had to stand on a seat and hold a slate up over his head. I was putting books away into a cupboard because I was the monitor and then, when I looked round, George was getting out of the window. It'd been up because it was a warm afternoon. So I told Mr Longbottom, 'George is gettin' owt o' winder, Mr Longbottom!'

He says, 'I have him, follow me, James.'

So I followed him across the road and George then had the teacher down. Mr Longbottom saw me looking down at him and said, 'Get him off me, James, pull him off, pull him off!'

I pulled him off and George got free and set off down Cockersdale as hard as he could go, and me and Mr Longbottom went back to the classroom and carried on tidying up. Mr Longbottom didn't bother with George much after that.

I finished school at fourteen; from twelve to fourteen we'd finish school back then. We'd go home at half past four from Board School. Some weeks we had afternoons at work and mornings at school and then the reverse. We used to have what they call piecework at band walk, and this piecework consisted of making what we called 'Hardings'. There were sixteen threads divided up into four. You ran down the walk, 200 or 300 yards, and you hung 'em on a piece of board; it had some bricks on for weight, and you set your machine off, spindles whizzing round, and you twisted the bands, and, when this board had got to a certain point, you'd to stop it with a cord, take 'em off, and as you were taking 'em off, you'd to put another four on, and you'd seventeen to do for your morning's work, two shillings and sixpence per week.

When I left school I stayed at band walk and worked full time on the drums and I earned nine shillings per week, and they used to give us a trip to Skegness or Bridlington. I worked on drums until I got too big and I got a job at the brick yard, Rushforth's. I drove a horse for a time. This horse used to stand, stop and fall on the floor, and the weight that I was pulling used to drag the horse back down to where the men were working. It had been doing this for many weeks and Mr Rushforth came down one day with a stick, and he saw it do it, and he says, 'Jim, 'ow long 'as that 'oss bin doin' that?'

Rushforth's Brickworks, Wakefield Road

I said, 'It's bin doin' it ever since I driven it!'

He says, 'Tek this stick, an' as soon as 'iver it starts, let it 'av 'un.'

I only had to do it once and it cured it.

I wasn't so happy at this job and I had an auntie who got my uncle to take me as an apprentice to a mason. I was seventeen and I had eight shillings a week and a shilling or two rise every year and we worked at Ardsley. I used to have to go on the five fifteen train, wait while it was daylight, start squaring flags until the rest of them came on a later train and then I used to go on while I caught a train at five twenty-five. I remember one Christmas Eve they'd gone home on an earlier train and left me squaring flags, it was frosty and a bit snowy and I had to stop until my train, and when I got to Ardsley station there was a plumber there that I knew, Mr Mason, and he were a bit fresh [drunk], but I wasn't bothered, so we got into the railway carriage and he was carrying on and I was laughing at him and we got snowed up. The Leeds train couldn't get up and we couldn't move 'til the Leeds train had come and we didn't get to Gildersome station until seven.

Mr Mason came to work with us; he was right to work for, a real special sort. There wasn't much plumbing work going. A time or two he'd let go of his temper and say such things.

Billy Monk kept pigeons and he used to get larks to sing at the pub. The ones that sang longest got prizes. He went up to Penfield Free with a young lark and he took some chaps with him, he went over the wall and asked them to stand on the footpath. 'I'll get it singin',' he said, 'and you lot just time it.' And while he was fiddling about this lark got away from him. This chap also kept pigeons; he had a little loft in the underdrawing in his house. He had a blue cock and he took some chaps on Saturday dinner time at Whit Saturday to look at it. His wife asked where he was going. 'I'm goin' to show 'em t' blue cock I bought.'

'I've just washed!' she says, 'Yer can go up but yer first man that comes down mucky'll get some long brush.'

They went up and had a look at this blue cock and as they were coming down Mrs stood there with a long brush ready, and Billy says to the others, 'When tha gits to t' ninth step, jump!' And they did, and she broke the brush trying to hit 'em. They all ran out laughing.

'Tha's won this match,' she says, 'but there'll be another.'

He was flying this pigeon in on Tuesday through Birkenshaw and we all stood waiting for the pigeon to come back, and she was wearing a white pinny, and she heard 'em saying 'Ee's 'ere!' and she waved her apron and wouldn't let the pigeon land, and so he lost the match.

'Now', she says to Billy, 'we're straight.'

We used to rent some land off a man for ten years. He was in partnership with two others. They were very funny people, the two of 'em, they were teachers and they were very 'near', all they could think about was saving money. They had two buckets, one at each side of the fireplace, and she used to put a bit of coal on, and if he thought she'd put too much on he'd take a piece off and put it in his bucket. The war was on and they had a big cellar and they asked me to go look at it. There were hundreds of bricks all piled up all round the cellar and on top of these bricks were packets of margarine with all dates on, she was saving it, and butter and sugar all with dates on. Some were last year's but she had it all in order so's she used the oldest first.

The old man fell into the fire, burnt himself, and they had to get the doctor and have the bed in the front room. I went to see how he was and she says, 'I can't keep 'im in bed, Jim, an' Doctor says 'e 'asn't to get up. What would you do?'

I says, 'Burn 'is britches!'

Without more ado she throws 'em on the fire and says, 'There, Fatha, you can't get up now.'

And that finished that job.

Nethertown chapel

I started my apprenticeship for Uncle Jim. He sent me to Nethertown chapel to wall a grave for a Mrs Topham. He gave me a lump of chalk as big as my fist, and we chalked out the grave. The next week he asked me where the lump of chalk was.

'I left it,' I says.

'Well, tha'd better go git!' he says.

'I can't,' I says. 'I'll 'ave to dig down.'

'Well, remember,' he says, 'if I gives thee summat tha' sticks to it. That chalk were useful.'

He chuntered all the way from Robin Hood to Wakefield.

Later that week I was building some chimney breasts and a man and a woman passed. The man wasn't so big, he wore a belt and had a trowel stuck in the side, and was swinging a brick hammer, and he also carried a monkey with him. A little woman walked at the side of him. He asked Uncle Jim if he could give him a starter [job]. Jim said no, but asked where he worked last.

'Leeds,' says the man. 'I'm makin' me way to Wakefield an' this is me wife an' we 'aven't no 'ome – I only carry t' monkey so far an' then make 'er walk t' rest.

'You don't want me, then?' he says to Jim.

'No,' says Jim.

Well, the man started cursing and swearing ...

John Nicholls used to be a trustee at church. He fell ill with lumbago and he lived just below the chapel. Dr Davidson was the doctor. The doctor sorted him out, but Mr Nicholls wouldn't get up and walk.

'You'll have to,' says Dr Davidson. 'If not I'm going to operate at three o'clock tomorrow.'

'What'll this operation consist of?' asks Mr Nicholls.

'Well, I'll boil the kettle, I'll lay you on your tummy and I'll pour boiling water down your back to where the lumbago is, and that'll be a cure. Your choice,' he says. 'I'll be here at three pm and if you're not up I'll do the operation.'

Next day when he arrived John was up. He didn't have to operate.

John Tover lived in a cottage; this man stood about six foot eight. He lived by himself. One of his jobs was to mend women's peggy tubs. He used to come up every morning – he never missed – with his leather apron on, a glass case on his back with sheets of glass, his putty and his hammer. He wore clogs and had a right bad cough, and every yard he'd 'aagh aagh aagh'. He'd walk everywhere – Howden Clough, Birstall, Batley. They wouldn't allow him on the train. Kids used to mock him until he chased them. They were frightened of him. He used to glaze windows.

We had a balloon ascent in the park when I was about nine or ten, and one of the men doing the ascent was a barber. He stayed at the Victoria. It was sixpence to go into the park. The balloon was silky grey with a basket at the bottom and sand bags – it was a lovely thing. They filled it with gas from a valve in the road. I had to deliver milk with my dad and I saw a man carrying a bag striding across Penfield to Howden bridge. The barber was wearing red knee britches – he was a real toff. He started messing around with the balloon and decided he wasn't going to go up. Everybody had paid their money and got real angry with the man and some started hitting him with the sandbags as he tried to escape and climb through the window into the Vic. Some of them, they took the basket off and the rest of the sandbags and let the balloon go. It rolled over and went over the ginger beer place, the Board School and down Nethertown. About a hundred followed it down and somebody was going to strike a match. Gas was coming out the balloon fit to smother you, and a man hit the balloon with a walking stick, tearing it, so they tore it up in strips and sold it for a penny a yard. The man I saw running across the field was the barber's partner, who was running away with the brass people had paid to go into field. The whole thing was a con.

Victoria Hotel and pub, Drighlington crossroads

I'd just got married when me and my brother took a job at Primrose Main for Sam Rushforth. Ten of us from the village were setting an engine bed in the pit yard and building a place into the pit bottom for an engine room. First day there a chap took us to look at our lodgings; first place he took us to was a barn, which the man was going to fill with beds for our lodgings. We told him he thought wrong if he thought we were staying there. I got a place with the deputy, who came from Drighlington, Ben Roberts. There were three of us in a bed and we all wore our top coats. Only the man who slept in the middle was warm, the others were all starved because there were no covers.

First day, me and Issac went down the shaft – they'd taken us tugs of lime and tugs of bricks down. The dayman, Gillespie, had been walling the side to hold the loose muck and he'd chalked on the wall 'Gillispie's gotten so far.' We hadn't been working half an hour when this fellow who we'd not seen before looked at us and asked where we came from and who'd sent us down. 'Mr Rushforth,' I says.

'You been in a pit before?' he says.

'Only little 'uns,' I says, 'not as big as this.'

'Well,' he says, 'you can't stop 'ere when I've gone, there's only one man left in this pit and who's going to look after you if you 'aven't been used to pit work?'

He was the bottom manager. Anyway, we stooped in, and used the lime up, and the bricks, and when we left I wrote 'Grayshon's got this far.' You had to crawl through a hole no bigger than a gas fire and pull your tackle up after you. Issac was a bit on the big side so I always let him go first, and sometimes he used to get stuck with the bucket. After we'd got through the hole you could stand up and then walk to the ladder and come out.

One day there, me and Issac were working when two young colliers passed us, cursing and swearing; they'd had a bad day. Then we heard this big crash. Some of the trains loaded with steel girders had jumped the points and crashed into the door we were working behind. Some deputies were at the lighting station further down the road and called out asking if we're alright.

'Yes,' I said, 'but we can't get out.'

'Don't worry about gettin' out', he says, 'as long as yer OK.'

There were six of us and it took them while seven at night to get us out. Next day some detectives came down and asked if we could identify the two young men we'd seen, but we couldn't. They thought the men had changed the points deliberately. As far as I know they never found out who it was.

One of the deputies had a bit of money saved and he wanted to build some houses. Sam Rushforth had taken the job but found out he couldn't do it. Sammy asked me if I could take it on, knowing I'd been to college for technical drawing and could draw plans.

'Aye,' I says, 'I'll tek it on if I can draw t' plans at 'ome.' I was newly married.

'Oh no,' says Sammy, 'you'll come here and work in my office at nights.'

So that's what I did, but every night Sammy'd come in and look at what I was doing and find fault. I've had enough of this, I thought. Anyway, going home on a night we'd to pass a pub and every time we passed this pub there were swords drawn at him, and these men didn't like Sam. I told him I'd finish the plans at home, and I did. He and his brother Willie had fallen out. Willie came one night and asked if I'd finished the plans. Sam wanted him to take them back and that I hadn't to sign my name on them. Willie, however, says, 'Tek no notice o' that, Jim, you sign 'em.' And he draws a ring in the middle of the plans and I signed my name.

Then Willie came back the next week and says I wasn't going to build this house. 'Good,' I says, 'I'm fed up wi' it,' and left. The plans were passed, but I don't know who built the houses or if they ever got built.

Jim Binns, a Drighlington lad, was a medium and used to have meetings and seances at the Mechanics Institute at Adwalton. One night they were holding a seance and the tablecloth moved and some screamed. Others thought they'd got in touch with the spirits. What they didn't know was Jim had a frog under the table.

The same Jim lived on Cobble Hill and used to do a bit of haulage. Jim had this mill contract and wanted to buy a horse from Jonathon Stead so he could meet the contract. Jonathon refused to sell him the horse he wanted. One day he changed his mind and Jim took the horse. Not long after Jim was seen carrying a pair of broken shafts. The horse had fallen and broken the shafts and Jim lost the job. Jim complained to Jonathon.

He said, 'Well, I knew it 'ad an 'abit o' fallin' asleep an' every fifth shovelful I used to throw it over t' cart on its 'ead and it used t' keep it awake. Throw every fifth shoveful on t' oss.'

Jerry Garfit lived in the village, and he'd no legs, and his brother Will was the surveyor. Jerry, he used to wear a billycock [hat] and clean the dross off the road. Jerry lived in a low cottage where the Midland Bank was. The dross had to be broken up at the side of the road and Jerry used to go on a little flat cart with four wheels on and two spiked canes, which he used to propel himself, and with hammers, and he used to sit on the pile of dross until dinner time breaking it up into small pieces. He had a pot sale in front of the White Hart. He used to start by giving you little bargains. I went one night to the sale and he put some grand ornaments up and asked two shillings for them. I bought them and left to come home. Next day I saw some mates that had stopped at the sale and asked how they went on. 'Tha got t' best bargain,' they said.

Harry Asherton had one of the best puppet [marrionette] shows there was and one of the puppets was called Yorkshire Bob. He wore a pair of clogs. He also had Dick Turpin and Black Bess. He also did plays and a man in the village used to take the actors in, so much a night, but didn't use to feed them. Jim Armitage was his name.

When I was a lad I heard 'Lakes of Killarney' sung. We had seventeen pubs in Drig; we used to start at Adwalton then come to the Unicorn at Three Lane Ends. You used to have to go up some steps. This woman used to come to Tong Street, her husband had tuberculosis. She used to wear a veil and she used to sing this song at the top of the steps. She was a soprano, a real good singer. When she'd sung she took her veil off and somebody would go round collecting money, all pennies.

Louie Hall, a cricketer, built a house from his benefit money down in Birstall.

There used to be a girl in Birstall called Molly Hall who had one leg; her brother had a pot round in Birstall: Harry. Molly had a monkey which used to steal stockings from washing lines and tennis balls from the tennis players. It got to be a bit of a nuisance. When she and her husband went to bed at night the monkey used to turn the radio on so they couldn't get to sleep.

The moor belonged to Mrs Day, who gave instructions that not a yard of the moor had to be sold. They used to come and collect rents for the little bits that had been taken off the moor and collect all the farm rents: Sam Grayshon's farm, Scott's and Ted's farm, a farm by the Congregation chapel and Chalner farm. On a certain day in the year the farmers used to take their rents to the Victoria Hotel. Mr Brown, a fine stout fellow with ginger hair, used to walk round the village when he was here and said all clothes posts had to be removed and if they weren't the people would be prosecuted. Jack Harrison got coal off the moor: sink a shaft, dig all the coal out around it, then dig another shaft and put in all the muck from the first shaft.

We had a bill poster called Henry Ellerton; he used to die the lamps out and light them and post bills on the hoardings. Henry's mother used to keep leeches and you could have one on, at three pence a time. She used to keep 'em in jars. If you'd a severe headache or such she used to put the leeches on until they'd filled with blood, then they'd drop off. Then she used to put 'em back in the jar. She kept 'em all in the bedroom on the windowsill.

Some of the houses in Drig had their sewage led into the old pit shafts. Some of them still go in shafts all over the place. The deepest seam was twelve yards, nearly forty foot. Where there is a seam there had to be an air shaft. We were once laying drains and the drain ran very near the threshold of the house. We lifted the flags up, they were about two inches thick, and found an air shaft underneath. The people living in the house had been walking on these flags for years and they could have collapsed into the shaft at any time. We had a word with the borough surveyor and we agreed not to tell the families. And we filled the shafts in. We even asked the bin men not to take the rubbish so we could use it to fill the shaft.

The White Hart hotel

Harry Suddick
1916–

My earliest memory is the district nurse coming to our house and my mother towering above me, sat on a potty. The reason the nurse came is because I was constipated! I was the only child; I had no brothers or sisters. We lived in a cottage, the address was Moorside Road. It had two rooms, a living room and a bedroom, it also had a cellar under the bedroom. I started school at the age of five and I can remember the teachers were Mrs Hetherington and a Mrs Muffit, and at seven years of age I had moved into standard one in the boys' school. The teacher there was Miss Clayton. The boys were segregated from the girls. Contact in school hours was strictly forbidden. Even looking over the wall was punishable with the cane. Mrs Blythe took standards two and three, Mr Dickenson took standard four, Mr Longbottom standards five and six and Mr Harrop, the head teacher, took standards seven and eight, and he was very strict. School days were interrupted at twelve for dinner.

It was at this time I had my right leg fractured. I had a compound fracture of the right thigh and the nurse said it was a miracle that I was able to walk again. I did it when a boy jumped on my back when I was thirteen. Football was my greatest passion.

My father was a coal miner at Howden Clough collieries and he seemed to be always at work.

I remember I had a pair of leather leggings for winter that were given to me; when on, they came from the ankles to just below the knees.

The games we used to play were flying kites, whip and top, and if you had a pork pie top you were special. Bully bowl is an iron ring about two foot in diameter and an iron stick with a hook or a ring to attach it to. If the ring split we would take it to the nearest blacksmith: there were loads in the village and surrounding area and they would repair it free of charge.

The transport in those days was horse and cart. Trams later started at Drig crossroads and went to Bradford, and then the West Riding Bus Company started a service from Wakefield to Bradford. Also B and M Transport bus company ran a service, and we also had a local service with a minibus from Drig crossroads to Morley Town Hall. This'd be a fifteen or sixteen seater and many a time in winter with the bad roads passengers had to get off the bus and push it up Bruntcliffe Lane.

I can remember once going to Blackpool on a day trip in a charabanc. The seats were the full width of the coach with a row of doors on each side, and then there was a canvas hood that had to be pulled over the top for bad weather. It ran from Birstall to Blackpool. The only other holiday I can remember is another a week's trip to Blackpool.

Bradford tram at the crossroads

I met my future wife, May, in Birstall. She was in a guide uniform, and it was her sparkling eyes and her kind of lopsided smile that attracted me.

I remember saying to myself at the time, this is the girl I am going to marry. My first job was at Scott Dudley Hill Ltd and May worked at Burnley and Sons, a spinning company. I worked seven am to five pm with an hour for lunch; Saturdays would be seven am to twelve pm. May's hours were the same as mine. I earned seventeen shillings and sixpence when I first started working.

After we were married we took our honeymoon to Skegness. We got a train from Drighlington and should have changed at Wakefield but we missed our connection so our first visit was to May's Auntie Florrie's at Branton. We were married in Gomersal parish church on 5 June 1937. We arrived at Skegness on a Sunday and the cost for the week's holiday was two pounds, seven shillings and sixpence, and the landlady gave us a reduction because we arrived a day late.

Our first marital home was a cottage on Moorland Road and it stood where the meeting hall is now. It had a large kitchen with a beautiful polished wood ceiling. You went up about four steps into a sitting room with a bedroom off to the left. There was a big cellar underneath the bedroom. We had a large garden with apple trees and a brick-built garage-cum-shed, no bathroom, and a dry toilet at the side of the garden. It was a very good cottage in the summer and we lived there for about eighteen months. In September 1939 we moved to Whitehall Road. We had no bathroom or toilet but there were three houses in the block and we bought all three and had toilets put in. But we had no bath. After we were married it was usual that wives gave up work. I was on a pretty good wage; I started work at the wire works in 1933, so when the war broke out I was in a reserved occupation working twelve-hour shifts, a week on days and a week on nights, and also spent the war years in the Home Guard. When war broke out I was earning about six pounds per week, which was a very good wage at that time. We had a daughter, Christine.

As I've said, my passion was football, but I also liked gardening. I started keeping bantams and rabbits as a hobby and finally had the garden full of hutches, and I used to show the bantams at various shows. I had some success with Light Sussex and White Leghorns. We used to grow all our vegetables, such as potatoes, carrots, cabbages, turnips, Brussels sprouts, and things like that. We also had a big apple tree in the garden.

When Christine went to school May took a part-time job: she started off at a millinery place in Bradford as an alteration hand. She worked there quite a number of years and then moved to Cleckheaton, and at that time we were moving from 199 Whitehall Road to 189 Whitehall Road. May asked for the day off and they wouldn't give her it, so she took it off and then they sacked her. Later on she got a job at the Yorkshire Egg Packers.

Egg Packers, Whitehall Road

After the war we couldn't get a joint of meat every week like we used to do and we had ration books. The sweet shop further up the road called Sykes's got a supply of bananas, and when Christine went for one he wouldn't let her have one because we didn't spend our sweet rations there. We spent them at May's sister's, so we never got the banana.

If I could change one thing, that would be I would never ever consider a job that works nights. I worked fifteen years on shifts of twelve hours, working seventy-two hours on nights one week and seventy-eight hours on days the following week. For fifteen years I saw very little of Christine. In her school days when I got home she was ready for bed, and when I was on nights I was always in bed during the day. Working nights is a dead loss.

You can't compare the village really as to what it was and what it is now. When I was little everybody knew everybody. Now it's like a transit camp, there's people come and go. They come out of Leeds and then they miss the noise and the traffic, I think. They're only here a few months and then they're off again. Nowadays there's hardly anybody in the village that I know; it's not a friendly village like it used to be, no shops hardly. When I was little there was a Co-op shop at Three Lane Ends, then there were a couple of houses, two sisters had a drapery, there was another shop on

Pearson's Yard and my grandmother lived on Pearson's Yard; on the other side of the opening was the greengrocer's owned by a man called Durrance, and then next door to him it was a kind of smallholding really, Speights; they had some stables at the back, and then there were a couple of houses and then Larvin's, a barber shop. That man committed suicide sat in a chair facing a big mirror, so that closed that down. The Larvins lived in the house next door and Joe Larvin carried on cutting hair, but you had to go to his house to have it cut. Next door to what was the barber's was Robertshaw and Melton's, on King Street. They were a general store, and a house next door, and then a butcher's, then an opening with a yard and houses at the back, some houses at the front ... the end one was Frank Thomson's chemist shop, but he wasn't a qualified chemist so he couldn't make prescriptions up, but if you had any illness you went and told him and he would make you a medicine up without you going to the doctor. Then there was an opening and the other side of that was Minz's pork butcher, who was a really good pork butcher. When we used to go there for roast pork we used to go with a basin, and we'd get gravy with the roast pork, and his pork pies and sausage rolls were marvellous. The story goes that during the war when troops were marching through the village, in the First World War, he'd be outside handing out pork pies and sausage rolls to the troops as they marched by. The butcher, Mr Minz, was a German man, but he had not been interned. Next to the butcher in King Street was a general purpose ironmonger's shop; it was Broscom and Kitson's. You used to be able to buy anything in the hardware line there. I used to have a cinematograph I got for a birthday from there. Now it's the Londis supermarket, but after the ironmonger's it became a chemist, then a television shop. Then after another house there was a small opening, and there was a fish shop, which is now a takeaway. Next to that was a row of houses. The house on the far end where Frank Thomson used to live is now occupied by David Totham. There was a row of houses back to back, then there was a field that is now Moorside Building Supplies. Then you come to the Black Bull. In the 1920s my granddad was the landlord there for a few years. There used to be a stable at the back where customers could leave their horse and trap when they went for a sup [drink]. Then there was a building that stands back, which was at one time occupied by Slack Bros. Then there was a row of houses and the first house used to sell sweets. There were one or two houses like that that used to sell sweets.

They had a counter just inside the door; you could buy cigs and pop there too. Then there was a wood building called Aveyard's paper shop for a lot of years. He eventually closed down and moved up Whitehall Road. Then there was a block of houses and then the Post Office, which has always been there all my lifetime. The house next to the Post Office, then an opening going down to Spring Gardens, then a wooden hut. I can remember it being a fish shop, a greengrocer's, which also sold wet fish. Then there was a cobbler's shop then there was a bank, the Midland, then there were fields. The house next to the bank was the bank manager's house. Up Whitehall Road at the Egg Packer freezer part, that building used to be a cinema showing silent films in black and white. It was run by a gas engine; you could hear it going 'phut phut phut' when it was showing films. The owners didn't come from the village. I can remember the park being opened in 1926.

The current pet shop on Whitehall Road has been a butcher's, a milliner's, a cobbler's and a joiner's shop before its present use. The two buildings at the crossroads, one was sweets and a tobacconist and the other was a plumber's shop. The front of the Barracuda was Naylor's, then there used to be a wood hut selling pie and peas and tripe, but I can't remember who owned it. The baker's shop which was attached to the Salvation Army was Smith's; they had their own big ovens and baked all their own stuff. There used to be a greengrocer's on the other side of the road where the doctors' car park is. The first part of the Co-op building used to be a draper's shop and at the end there was a butcher's. The other side of the building was a Co-op tailor's shop; next to the Trawler fish shop there used to be a boot and shoe shop. Below the bowling green used to be Edison's sweet boilers.

Drighlington had its own council up to I think 1939. When Morley took over they spoilt the moor. The moor was full of little hills and hollows here we could have lots of fun as children, hiding in and around the place. But they levelled it and filled Sally Dicks' pond, but the pond was fed by a natural spring and the ground behind the meeting hall is always soggy. When they levelled the moor out on Moorside Road they put in a pitch and putt course, but it was hardly ever used. It should have been, but nobody in the village wanted it.

There's been a lot of changes in the village. There used to be a lot of rhubarb grown here where Fairfax Avenue is, and Kingsdale Gardens. They also grew rhubarb where the bypass is now. Hammond Crescent used to be a football field. We had two old trams for changing rooms. Lawrence Holdsworth started a sports and social club and he was the first man in this area to pay his workforce holiday pay, and he was also the first employer to give two weeks' annual holiday with pay. He had a club foot, but it didn't stop him playing tennis. He organised the Home Guard during the war and part of the building that used to be Farnell's saw mills was used as the headquarters. When Lawrence Holdsworth's son was twenty-one he took us all to Blackpool, where we had a meal in the Winter Gardens. He was a very good employer but he detested trade unions. At the bottom of West Street there was a spinning mill which employed a lot of the village and Slack Bros was a big employer in horsehair manufacturing. When the bottom fell out of that market he turned to plastic products. They invented their own machinery for doing plastics. There was also a spinning mill on Moorland Road on the site of Southgate Lighting. In 1960 a lot of houses were condemned and a lot of the village was destroyed.

During the war there was a raid on Bradford and it was always thought that these bombers had lost their way and it was a matter of getting rid of the bombs before they flew home. They started dropping incendiaries over Drighlington and shrapnel was exploded all over the place. We were stood inbetween two buildings at Holdsworth's, and you could feel the shrapnel whipping past you. We saw fires springing up just outside Drig railway station and ran to put the fires out, and we were trampling on unexploded incendiary devices. We were lucky, because nobody got hurt.

Slack Bros Ltd, King Street works

Artillery marching through Adwalton, 13 August 1914

David Eastwood
1932–

I was born in 1932 and I was born on Tong Street, just down the road, and we moved to an old property just up the field off Wakefield Road. My father had some greenhouses which were quite big, and a rhubarb shed, and as children we used to play around the sheds, but as time went by we used to wander off for hours on end, but you were never out of the sight of someone who knew you. The milkman would come twice a day, the coal man came, the ice cream man, the pop man, and in winter the ice cream man would come with his pies and his brown peas. I remember them because they took the place of sweets. There were five children in our house. I have two sisters and two brothers. And then Shangri-La appeared on the horizon in the shape of Oakwell Road and Fairfax Avenue, and we moved out of our house that had gas lights, a tin bath and outside privy to a magnificent mansion with three bedrooms, electric lights, inside bathroom and toilet. Marvellous, that was, but there was part of the freedom of the fields that we had that was disappearing fast.

Our old house used to have two rooms upstairs and two down with a dry cellar. Most folks' cellars flooded in Drig but ours only flooded when it rained, as it came through the roof. We had a stone sink with a side pan fire and a hole in the ground called a dry midden. It wasn't until 1941 that we had a flush toilet and that was heaven. In 1939, when Drighlington went under Morley, Drig had the biggest number of dry middens in the country. In those days in the thirties all Drighlington was fitted with gas lights because it had its own gas works and the shareholders were the property owners of Drighlington. The six cottages on Wentworth Terrace where we used to live were formerly owned by Miss White and one of the Gills of Wakefield and his sister used to come and collect the rents. In 1939 they fitted street gas lights. They did away with the paraffin lamps and in the houses put gas mantles for lights, but they were easily broken. To see the demise of candles upstairs and the shouts from mother not to burn the house down was a good thing and a modern thing, of course.

I remember my grandma, she was quite a character, and she lay in her sick bed and never liked the gas light. Her niece lit the gas light for her one year after installation. I could never understand it. My mother worked as a weaver and my dad was a market gardener but he spent some time down the coal mines. He was at the Bruntcliffe pit in the 1929 strike and to keep the new mill going on Drighlington moor they even dug part of the moor up for coal, and that's how they kept the mills in Drig going throughout the strike. All the miners' wives worked there. When my father got laid off from

Oakwell Road

the pit, he somehow got a job with an uncle of mine at the mill at Girlington, and they used to cycle all the way out to Girlington for the half past six start. My dad couldn't handle the mill for some reason or other. He'd had a go at it before when he got married but he went back to the coal mine. In the 1930s they did all manner of things to earn money, and of course he did a bit of farming in Drighlington. At that time there was a lot of rhubarb, and he went into market gardening. After the Second World War Dad and his two brothers opened greengrocery shops in the village, which they maintained for quite a few years.

I remember as a child I used to like football and cricket and we used to climb trees and there used to be a dip by the second roundabout going to Birstall. We used to call it the Hell Hole. It progressed to being filled in as a landfill tip. There were some marvellous trees there that we could swing off, and you could get a good swing on them, or if you could climb high up and borrow a rope off somebody, and you slung it up at a high level, it was marvellous, that. Through the seasons there were quite a few grouse there and it was wonderful to hear the mechanical 'craw, craw, craw' as they were in the bracken. We played football for hours on end until the ball got punctured. When I was twelve the Second World War was still going on. There was nothing to buy in the shape of footballs. You could buy puncture outfits, of course. The balls always got punctured regularly, every night, because your fields were surrounded with hawthorns and the leather casing wore thin, so we pulled the rubber inner out and we got the puncture repair kit out and repaired it in the evening dark. Sometimes you could borrow a cricket bat from somebody's uncle; I managed to get a cricket bat and some wickets off my uncle who lived at Birkenshaw, so that was a real treasure, though I never achieved much at cricket. I had an accident with my arm and that threw me off cricket.

We didn't have a holiday away at all until I was fourteen years old, and that was the first time my parents took us away. As a young child my auntie and uncle took me to Blackpool three years on the go, but as I got older they took the young 'uns. We went to some friends of my parents at Derby and they lived near to the river, and it was a thoroughly enjoyable time, but other than that I never went away with my parents at all. We had Sunday school trips though, and they were the highlight of the year. You saved up for it, a shilling or two shillings a week to pay for the train journey from Drighlington station to Cleethorpes, somewhere like that. Although we didn't have much, we ate OK, as we had pigs, hens and a small market garden business.

I met my good lady at Morley Picture House, Saturday evening, second house; you'd to book for the second house – it was very popular – and 'course the young men and women were parading up and down Queen Street. At the time I was short of a bit of money 'cos I'd bought a motorbike and that was taking a bit of running, but I met her and she kindly offered to share her sweets, which was good as they were rationed. In our house my mother bartered sweet coupons for food coupons, same as she bartered food coupons for clothing coupons. All families did at some time or other. Mind you, if you could get a bit of cloth out of the mills then they'd make a pair of trousers or something like that, hand sewn mostly. My good lady can even remember the film that was showing. I can't, but it was *The Three Caballeros*. I think they were poor sweets, they weren't Quality Street: they were Spangles. And that's fifty-seven years ago!

I was a joiner all my life, I served three years in the army, national service, plus a bit, and then worked in a shop fitter's and then worked for myself for thirty years in the village. My wife worked at Wood and Baxter's in Leeds but she didn't like it 'cos she hated travelling all the way on the bus. She got a job at the fent warehouse in Morley, which was just below where Lloyds bank is today.

I was in the army when we got married and we went to Torquay for our honeymoon and we went on the motorbike, of course. After the traditional church wedding and afternoon ham tea at the church hall – teetotal – we set off south and of course we were heading down the old A1, getting towards Doncaster, and I flew through this junction and all of a sudden there was a screeching of police cars and everything. He said, 'Do you know you've just come through a stop sign?'

'Where?'

He said, 'There!'

I said, 'I never saw it.'

And I'm not exaggerating, but it was twenty foot square.

'Where you going?' he says.

I says, 'We're going on our 'oneymoon.'

'Ha ha, what a laugh,' the policeman said.

'I can prove it.'

'Can you?' he said. 'Right, we'll book you.'

He rode twenty yards down the road, then rolled back and said, 'We'll let you off this time – but we'll watch for you coming back.'

Anyway, the honeymoon was alright in Torquay; we did a lot of miles, but the bike broke in two coming back, the frame cracked, but I managed to get it welded and I got home. She came on the train with all the luggage. We lived in Morley when we were first married in a nice semi-detached; my wife liked it, but I didn't because nobody talked to me, so I got myself an allotment to give me some freedom and to have people to talk to, and so, in spite of working full time in the joinery, I spent some time on this allotment. We moved back to Drighlington in 1963. We bought this house off Tom Burniston. He was a teacher and his wife was a teacher at Drighlington School. It stood on what was a smallholding and we cleared the land and built a bungalow for my mother-in-law. When Margaret's mother died, my mother and father moved in, and lived there quite a while.

I remember when I was a lad that I did something that I wasn't supposed to do, and of course I always remember this. Keith Roper was with me. We climbed some apple trees and they were quite big trees at that time. They hadn't been pruned for years and they were just ready, these apples. We climbed up and it was dark, and the man who lived there, Mr Raby, came strolling round the front garden and we were up the tree and he had his dog and it was making a fuss and I didn't know what was going to happen. Anyway, we were lucky that evening, and we got away with it. One of the daftest things we did was climb trees, and there were some big ones in Miss White's garden. Now, Miss White's garden was out of bounds to everybody as she was a right terror, but these trees were ripe for climbing. We got in and were climbing along this branch to see how far to the end we could go when it snapped. Where the branch had snapped it left a big white scar, so we threw the branch over the hedge, got a bucket and mixed some mud up and put it over the big white scar to try and disguise it, but it didn't work. We got into trouble for that off our parents, but Miss White never found out who it was.

I remember a man called Gypsy Smith (he had a family); he used to disappear down the fields for a couple of days at a time. He would take two sticks with a bar across and light a campfire to roast a rabbit for his meals. I can remember that. As I said, he would stop for forty-eight hours, then go home.

I remember one time, there was a cup tie replay at Elland Road, and me and some mates bunked off school to go watch it. We caught the bus down there. The next day when we went to school the teacher called out, 'Hands up all of you who went to the football match yesterday.' Nobody owned up, but he said, 'Well, I got all your names from the bus conductor anyway.' So we stepped forward then and we all got the stick as punishment.

If I could change one thing today, it would be respect for other people, not fancy people but for people who lived a good life, did their best for others. I think that respect for others was something that I always admired and somehow today it seems to be missing, and I think I would try to get this respect for other people back somehow. There seems to be a greed today that wasn't there then. You shared what you had.

Geoff Clayton
Deceased

I went to Drighlington School and left at fourteen. In those days we'd to walk and walk back at dinnertime 'cos there were no school meals. You took sandwiches if you wanted lunch at school. When I left school, I went to work at Dale Farm and I was there for about nine months, and then I worked at Stead's rhubarb growers at Farnley, and then when I was sixteen I went to work in Robinson's garden shop in Leeds. From there I went at nineteen to work in Booth Bros textile mill.

At Robinson's in summer we started at half eight on a morning and worked until seven Monday to Thursday, and Friday we finished at eight. Saturday we finished at nine. Wednesday was half-day closing, though, actually. In winter, we opened at nine o'clock but still stayed open until the same times at night. I started with ten shillings and when I left pay was two pounds and five pence. On the buses at that time you got a pass that cost three shillings for a week, which was three pence a journey, and the conductor snipped you in and out by the date. I left because my pals didn't have Wednesday afternoon off and I didn't have Saturdays off and so I couldn't go anywhere with my pals. I had to go to the pictures on my own.

When I went to Booth's I worked roughly fifty hours per week and then, the last eighteen months before I went into the forces, I started at half six on a morning until quarter to nine at night for five nights, and Saturday morning half six to twelve, and I hadn't four pounds to take home.

I went into the forces in April 1940 and I was called up to the searchlights at Norton Manor barracks, Taunton, Somerset. I was there until Dunkirk and then I was transferred to Gloucester aircraft factory and was there all through the Battle of Britain until October when I went to Blackdown Camp at Aldershot for posting. I got posted to Blackpool until March of the following year when I went to Liverpool and learned to drive at the Army School of Motoring. The first vehicle I learnt to drive was a Comer, then a Bedford. After a month I was sent back to the regiment and put into troop. I was in B Troop Royal Artillery. The regiment had been a static anti-aircraft regiment but was going mobile – that's why I learnt to drive. I moved to Rainford, St Helens, until they started to bomb all the cathedral towns and we were packed up, moved to Truro and also guarded Falmouth, which was a big port. After ten months we went on a battle course in Hertfordshire and then to Blandford Camp, Dorset. Three days before Christmas there were no rations, so they sent us all home en bloc until the New Year. At Blandford we started training – getting vehicles, guns and equipment on to landing craft. We got concrete blocks from Portland Bill in Dorset, built a dry landing craft in the camp, and started to practise loading and unloading equipment.

We then went to the Little Orme at Llandudno to practise firing guns at targets during the day, and using searchlights at night to fire at targets two miles out to sea. Next, to Scotland, where we practised getting on and off a landing craft in the Clyde, then a two-week course at a dry land ship called HMS *Armadillo*, where every morning we had to parade in best battle dress under the flag. At this camp there was a wooden jetty out into the loch, which we thought was for landing supplies. After three or four days we were given lifebuoys, which you had to blow up yourself. You had to walk to the end of the jetty and if you didn't jump you were pushed in and if the lifebuoy didn't work properly there was always somebody with a boat hook to fish you out. While we were there we did a night landing and also a thirty-mile route march – that was very rough. We went to Tenby and Saundersfoot in South Wales for about a month to do the actual loading and unloading of ammunition and vehicles. Cardigan Bay in South Wales was next; we went on a firing course.

Eventually we came back to the south coast at Horsham to prepare for the invasion. The night before the invasion the big boats with the commandos and landing craft set sail about ten at night and we left the Solent at eight the next morning. We had got halfway across the channel when we saw dozens of light landing craft that the commandos had landed with coming back on the following tide. And I landed on the night of D-Day at place called Riva Bella on Sword Beach. The different beaches all had a name: Utah was American troops, Gold Beach was British and Canadian troops. Sword Beach was on the mouth of the River Orne, ten miles away from a place called Caen. The Germans occupied Caen for a good couple of months before we got them out. We were on the sand dunes for two weeks before we could move inland. The night before Caen fell there were bomber raids, which turned night into day, and we dropped leaflets urging the Germans to surrender.

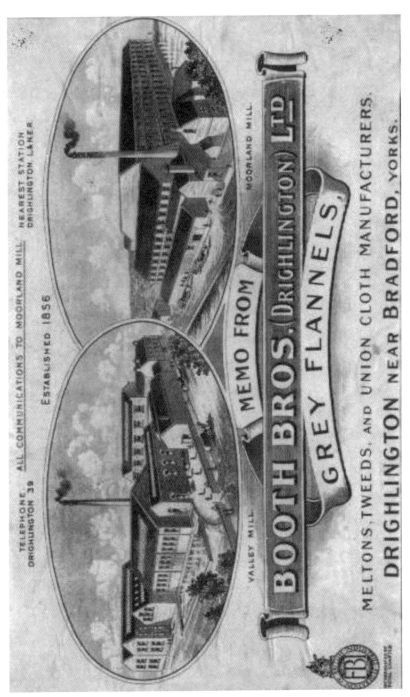

Old Booth Bros letterhead, used between circa 1916 and the late 1940s

Albert R Barmby
1924–

Albert travelled to Drighlington in October 1944. He now lives in the USA.

On one of my days off I went to the officer of the day and asked for a pass. You see, my father was born in a town called Drighlington in West Yorkshire. It was at the crossroads of a road leaving Bradford and a road from Leeds. All I knew about the area was that I could get to that town from the city of Bradford. I had checked out the Blackburn train depot for train schedules and prices. I explained all this and got my pass.

I left on an early train for Bradford. I do not recall having to make a change going over. I remember having to locate the proper class car and the side doors ... our American train cars are all what the English call corridor cars. However, some corridor cars had compartments in England. The American cars generally did not, except some special coaches. As a result I rode with a number of English persons who became friends rather quickly.

After a short time we reached Bradford. I left the train and found an American type of booth. The English lady there told me how to get to Drighlington. After a little walking, I found the tram for Drighlington. I do not recall if it was a rail tram or a bus tram. Again, after a very short ride, the tram dropped me off in Drighlington village. It was just like pictures I had seen in books, with attached stone houses, cobblestone streets and stone sidewalks. A little walk down the street I found the parish church. As I came up the walk the vicar came out in a hurry for some event. I explained my purpose and gave him my name and military address. I never got his name, unfortunately. Then I went back to the street to ask around about my ancestors. I promptly met the local constable; he was assigned to Drighlington but had trained at Riding Academy. He was assigned from some precinct to this local town for the day. We shared news and since I was looking for Norton as another family name he stopped a small auto with several persons in it. He asked them to give me a ride down to the crossroads, which was about a mile. At the crossroads was the Norton tannery [possibly a shoe shop/repairers]. I went into the office and explained my visit's purpose. My request caused quite a stir. It seems half the people in the tannery were named Norton! Much as I tried I could not locate any who might have known my grandmother. So, I left and returned to the town centre.

As it was, when I got there, the constable was still on duty. Since it was after lunchtime he took me to a small tea shop and he had a hot tea while I had chocolate and a cruller [pastry]. It was like eating in someone's front room! Tea shops didn't exist in my town but my mother's mother had one in Tewksbury, Massachusetts.

Later, I took the tram back to Bradford and made my way to the train station. My ticket back involved a transfer at a train station which I remember as Burnley. The train was blacked out, but a lady in my compartment was getting off there and she was going on to Blackburn. Thanks to her I boarded the proper train and made it back to Blackburn safely. In spite of the blackout I also made it back to the barracks with no problems. After all, I used to patrol that area nights! I checked in with the officer and then went to the officer of the day's office to turn in my pass. Since he did duty for the whole day, he was the same one who was on duty that morning. I spent the next half hour telling him about my travels and then turned in my pass. Next I went to see the mess sergeant. The reason he had such an interest in my travels was simply because most of us had never travelled abroad. A lot of us had never left our own state until we were drafted! Or, as in my case, had enlisted. You see, I had three years of college with my military training in addition. The officers had mostly just finished college with an extra year of training. Our age differences were usually about two or three years, so we had a lot in common. Half our battalion were three-year college men and half were stolen from Bell Telephone Company! That latter bunch were old enough to be our fathers.

In short, it was an eventful and different day for a guy who had barely left his country. The English people were very helpful and genuine in their help. And that's how I remember the Blackburn and Drighlington train trip.

Albert on his horse, Ben, in 1946

Annie Scott
1913–

I was born in 1913 at New Mill, where my dad was the engine man. I started school aged five and I left when I was fourteen. To get to school I used to run up and down over the pit tip – it was a hill. When I left school, I went to work at Brooks mill, weaving. I earned twenty-five shillings per week and worked from half six in the morning until half five at night – long days, five day a week. I had to give up work to look after my mother, who was poorly.

For entertainment there used to be the little picture house up Whitehall Road. I used to go three times a week. It was silent pictures, and Ivor used to play the piano. It was always full.

I went to church all my life. I had a school friend – Doris Garforth – and she went to Moorside chapel and she asked me to go to a sausage and mash supper. I'd never been before so I went, and I met Harry, he went there, and that's where I started to go, because Harry was there. I don't go anywhere now as I can't hear or see very well.

I got married in 1942. I got married on Monday afternoon and he went away on Friday to Burma. I didn't see him again for five and a half years. It was a long time. While he was away, I lived with my mother. My grandfather and uncles were all mill engineers. My grandfather worked at Barker's on Asquith Avenue in Morley and Uncle John was at Watson's up Fountain Street. Uncle Dennis was down Bruntcliffe Lane, Uncle Milton was at a mill behind the Queen pub in Morley, and Uncle Lionel was at Park mills. They were all engineers except Uncle Ben, and he was a plumber. My dad worked at Glen mills before he came to Drighlington.

I spent a lot of time in Morley. I used to go on the puffer [train]. We used to go to Grandma's on a Saturday afternoon. Shops were open until nine pm. My mother used to go with my auntie – her sister – shopping. I used to stop with my grandmother. She was a little fat woman and my mother and auntie were right thin. My grandmother couldn't put me on her knee, she was too fat.

Mother had a number at Morley Co-op but she used to shop on Wednesday at Drig Co-op. There were lots more shops in Drig then than there are today. They spoilt Morley with this White Rose Centre – they should never have built that. When I was younger, I would have like to have lived in Morley, but not now – they're all dead. I used to think it was lovely when trams used to come down Queen Street. We hardly ever used the bus, we always went by tram.

When Harry came back he worked at Binks at Morley. There was a sweet shop at the top of West Street – Edie Walker's, and she had a brother that had a joiner's shop at top of West Street. He used to make coffins. In fact, he made my father's coffin. Dad died in 1930.

There was once an accident at the mill. The fly wheel broke, and ooh, my dad was in a right mess – he could've been killed. There were two wheels in the foundation with teeth round and the wheel fitted into them. He knew it was sounding funny, and he ran down all the steps to get out. He was never right no more, it was the shock. They never give you anything for shock.

We played with dollies and skipping ropes, whip and top, shuttlecocks ... kids these days grow up too quick! I wish we could go back to those days, but not war days. Harry was in the East Yorkshire Regiment. He finished up as a sergeant. It was terrible, all the years when he was away. We did the best we could with rationing. We managed. It was tuppence halfpenny for a fish.

Brian Furniss
1932–

I was born in June 1932. My earliest memory is walking down to Batley with my dad to the dole office – about 1935. We walked from Field Head Lane to Batley because we couldn't afford the bus fare. I have three sisters, and I was spoilt. Dad was a general labourer on a farm, on Tommy Brooksbank's farm, Hill Top, at Birkenshaw.

My dad got ten shillings a week to pay rent, to feed and clothe us. Some used to go to draw the dole in the morning and some in the afternoon. In 1939 I was seven and my dad got a job delivering coal from Howden Clough Coal Company on Gelderd Road. The war was just starting and there was a field close to the pit and the Ministry was going to take over the field to grow corn. The boss knew my dad worked on a farm and asked him if he would take the field over, two acres. If he did they'd convert some of the offices into a house for us. 'Carry on working during the day for me and just do the field evenings and weekends,' he said, and that's what we did. We all had to help. My older sister had got married but her husband was in the forces so she'd come back home. We'd no tractor, no animals, so we had to borrow a horse from the farm across the road on the condition that at harvest time we helped get the hay in.

Howden Clough Colliery

We grew turnip, potatoes, cabbage, cauliflower, peas, beans, the lot. We'd to work to make it pay but we also used to live off it. We'd also poultry and ducks, which I had to feed, then on a Friday evening I'd go out with my dad collecting coal money. We'd be out on Friday until nine and then on Saturday morning. Two bags of coal were six shillings and four pence. He used to do one house and I'd do another until I got to know the round. If he was off sick I'd go out on a Friday and do the round from Birstall to Gomersal. I don't remember anybody not paying. There were other people collecting as well, one was Mrs Harrop. It was ages before I found out that she was a knocker-up [she woke people up so they could get to work on time] and she used to go round on a Friday collecting money from the people she'd knocked up during the week. She used to knock on the bedroom window with a stick.

We lived in a terrace house on Field Head Lane: we'd only two bedrooms. We'd a water closet in Field Head Lane, which was across the yard, and we shared with a neighbour, but when we lived on Gelderd Road we'd a dry midden. Every Saturday morning it was washed and scrubbed and the scouring stone put on the flags.

We didn't have a holiday as such but the Sunday school had a trip once a year from Drighlington station, and we had a day out at Cleethorpes. Easter and Whitsuntide we used to go to Cockersdale woods as a family and that's all we could afford. People today don't realise how hard it was.

I met my wife at the mill. I went to work there in 1946. I went into the Royal Pioneer Corps in 1950, and I was a drill instructor, and in 1953 I was involved in the Coronation. I got a letter saying I'd to go to a tailor for a uniform. I'd to give a paper and they had to tick all the boxes and measure me; then I'd to go to the hatter's to be measured for a hat; then I'd to go to be measured for boots and for gloves; and then I had to return the paper; and then I went to Wrexham, where it was all ready for me. There were only twenty-four chosen. We got there Friday afternoon and trained all week and they brought a group of Mauritian Pioneers over who'd been training for six months. We had to get up to their standard in about a week, so we drilled all Whitsuntide until eight at night. We were part of the parade. We went down on the Saturday morning before the Tuesday parade and stayed at Olympia to rehearse, until our arrival in the main hall was dovetailed. We all had to arrive together and the Tuesday morning we had to go to Buckingham Palace. We were actually at Buckingham Palace when it came over the tannoys that the Queen had been crowned. We weren't allowed drinks; we'd a couple of sandwiches and a bar of chocolate – that's all we could have – they didn't want anybody wanting to go to the toilet. It was brilliantly organised. We set off marching; we only saw the men in front of us, nothing of the rest of the parade. We marched back to Olympia and there was rum laid on for us. I didn't drink so I didn't have any. I was annoyed that we never got a medal. Only a few years ago I was in Scotland and looking in a display cabinet and saw a Coronation medal so I wrote and asked if I could have one. I got a letter back saying there were only five issued per regiment and officers had the first choice. So I bought a replica, which I have at home, but it's still disappointing.

We went to Cleethorpes for a week on our honeymoon and our first home was on Grayshon Street, the same house we've lived in for fifty-two years. We rented it to start with. The family that owned it lived in Hammond Crescent and we paid fifteen shillings a week. Unfortunately, the daughter of the family died when she was five, after an operation for tonsillitis, and then shortly after her mother committed suicide. The father moved to the other side of Leeds and asked if we'd buy the house rather than him trail over every week for the rent, so we bought it for £425, which was a lot of money. We didn't buy outright: we paid rental purchase.

I think I was affected by the war years because I still don't waste stuff. I don't eat exotic foods; I'm still happy with jam and bread – that's what I was used to as a child. We hadn't much money, in fact we were poor, but we had a loving home and our parents looked after us and to me that's far more important than money.

I don't think I'd change anything in my life – I'm very happy. I worked from fourteen to sixty-five and I've had a happy life. I worked in the mill forty-eight hours a week. We started at seven in the morning until six at night five days a week, and earned roughly two pounds per week. But if somebody was off – your partner on the machine – you got two shillings a day extra, ten shillings a week extra, which was a lot of money. I worked for Barron's mill and they closed in 1960 and Fred Dickinson from Morley took over until 1966, and they sold out to AW Ainsworth at Stanningley, and I worked with them driving a works bus picking people up at Drighlington, taking them

Barron's mill from across the moor

over there and bringing them back, for three years. Then Brooks wanted a warehouseman who lived in the village, and I worked there twenty-eight years. The mill I worked in made cloth for car head linings – we supplied Rover, Morris and Rolls Royce, but I think theirs was for inside the boots. We also made cloth for children's school blazers, duffle coats and the last twenty-odd years we made bunting, which was used for flags. We sent this all over the world. Thousands and thousands of metres was sent away every week. I was cloth inspector in the warehouse. We sent a lot to Norway, Sweden and Denmark. We made a lot of flags for the Ministry, the navy ... We used to save all the white cloth which was discoloured, spoilt, or stained or damaged, and every so often the Ministry would ask for white cloth for planes to use as target practice, so we sent that, so we never wasted any. Most of it was sent to Scotland.

We worked from seven in the morning until six at night. There was no canteen, and we mashed tea. During rationing two people would mash tea for the whole floor. There used to be tea and sugar in tin containers on each floor and you daren't lose or waste it. At half eight there'd be a shout of 'Tea up!' Nobody ever washed their hands; they wiped them down their overalls or on a bit of waste and then ate their sandwiches, but I never remember anybody being sick. We used to go to Janet Lambert's shop at Three Lane Ends on a Thursday for sandwiches, and she'd give us a penny for every delivery, so if ten people wanted sandwiches you got ten pence. Mr Sherwin had a fish shop and he used every morning to go to Bradford fish market with an enamel bucket for his fish. We used to go on a Friday.

CB Brook and Co Ltd (Brook's mill), Moor Top

At half past six in the morning at Gildersome crossroads there was as much traffic then as now. Coal wagons from Bradford used to race through the lights; they'd to get to the pit first because they needed two loads and if they got there late and were at the back of the queue they only got one load. Buses from Doncaster brought girls to work in the mills. They couldn't get the labour in Morley so they brought the girls in from the mining districts. The war had just finished and a lot of people didn't come back into the mills. Men had learnt trades in the forces and educated themselves so they didn't want to come back into the mills. But a lot of cloth was needed and the mills in Morley were working until eight every night. There were permanent signs up for vacancies and if you fell out with the foreman at one mill you could walk straight into the mill next door. There was rivalry but there were lots of laughs over things that don't happen now. Weavers would sing at the top of their voices, paper lads would whistle. I remember once we had a fuddle – a party. Two bottles of beer were left over and someone hid them to drink in the canteen next morning. Alf Taylor had seen where the bottles had been hidden, and after the women had gone home he told some other men who retrieved them, drunk the beer and filled the bottles with cold tea, put the tops back on and put them back in the hiding place. They were steaming! If a burler reported a weaver for bad work, very often at night they'd sew his sleeves up. I wouldn't want to change and go back to then, but the older workers looked after you and the people were like families, they'd worked there that many years. If you knew one you knew them all, and that's how you'd know people in the village. Wherever you walked you knew somebody. People stayed in the district. You knew everybody's pedigrees.

Barker's Buses loaf tins never left anybody. If you were waiting at a bus stop you'd get on that bus. They used to say 'Pass down, pass down,' and people squashed up; that many people that sometimes someone would fall out of the back door. If you were late to work he'd drop you outside the mills. They ran from Drighlington to Lee Fair, and all the time, not just work time. They say the drivers made as much as the bosses, but not all the money went in the bag. One for you, one for me. If you weren't in the mill at seven in the morning you'd to go past the timekeeper and you got your wages docked. We were lucky 'cos the foreman came at quarter to eight. They were hard but happy times, and everyone mucked in.

When we were kids we all played together and, although I guess we fell out from time to time, there were no violent squabbles like there are these days. In those days nobody had anything so it was a level playing field.

Our holidays at the mill were Easter Monday and Tuesday, Whit Monday and Tuesday, a week at Morley Feast, Christmas Day and Boxing Day, so you looked forward to the holidays. There were always special trains to Blackpool.

When I came here in 1946 there were cattle on the moor all summer from morning 'til night and they ate all the grass. We'd rabbits, hares, skylarks, and now they've gone. He'd take the cows back at tea time for milking. But nobody ever stole them.

Drighlington train station

The 'loaf tin' bus at the crossroads

Christine Day
1940–
Cub Scouting in Drighlington

I was in the guides from about twelve or thirteen years old. Mrs Pinchon, who ran the cubs in Drighlington in 1954, she started the cubs in the early 1950s, and George Pinchon, her husband, ran the scouts. One day she asked, could any one of the guides come down to give her a hand with the cubs because she had more cubs than she could cope with. I started off helping her, and being Baloo and then Bagheera: Baloo is the bear and Bagheera is the black panther. [Cub scouting traditionally has adopted ideas from Rudyard Kipling's *The Jungle Book*, and adults are often known by the characters' names.] In 1962 I took over as Akela [the cub leader].

We've been in various places for our headquarters. The rooms above the stables of the vicarage, the old cycle headquarters on Bradford Road, now gone, the Mechanics Institute on Wakefield Road, now gone, and the Liberal Club on King Street, which we were allowed to use as long as we cleared it. It was completely full of those old iron club-footed chairs and tables and we went round the village asking people if they would take them, and some did. We had to smash the rest of them up for scrap. Just think what they'd be worth now. We went into the paint shop at the bottom of Whitehall Grove, we went to the school, and the Barracuda was the last place we were in. Then the villagers were asked if they would buy a brick each for a pound. David Slack instigated this, because his daughter was in the guides and the guide hut was becoming in a bit of a bad state, so he thought it would be a good idea if the village had a guide and scout headquarters.

I was in the cubs from 1953 and Akela from 1962 to 1989. Miss Phillips was the head teacher when I was at school. She must have kept tabs on me as when my daughter went with the scouts to North Africa she actually donated some money towards the cost. They had an expedition across the Sahara, but initially it was to help the blind in Marrakesh. We both went, my daughter and I, to show Miss Phillips all the photographs and it was lovely to see her after all these years. I'd left school down there in 1951 and gone to Batley Girls' Grammar School, so I didn't see much of her after that. She looked exactly as I remembered her.

Barracuda Youth Club, Station Road, before conversion to a private house

Mr Lionel Adams was the group scout leader for years and then later Michael Garner. The new headquarters was built by leaders, local businesses, friends and relatives, and a Mrs Forbes actually gave us the piece of land that it was on. The actual HQ was opened by David Slack, who was the chairman in 1978, and, as I said, he was the original instigator who gave everyone a push to get our own headquarters. The original neckerchief for the Drighlington scouts and cubs was all one colour of green, but it was changed to gold with a black edge for a new start in the new HQ, and is the colour of the neckerchief now.

Scouting has altered over the years with new ideas: badges, rules and regulations. These had to be tightened up to protect the leaders as well as the children. The HQ took two and a half years to build. An awful lot of people helped to build it, too many to mention, and were invited to the opening day. Some of the bigwigs came. It is so difficult when you are trying think of something that was so many years ago and get it accurate!

Barracuda Youth Club after conversion

Policing in Drighlington in the Mid to Late 1960s

Police station: Bradford Road, Drighlington.

Personnel: one sergeant, five constables.

Duties: sergeant responsible for policing Drighlington and Gildersome; two constables at Drighlington and three at Gildersome.

Village bobby at Drighlington: ex-guardsman, six foot three tall, six seven with helmet, always worn at an acute angle on his head, did not believe in arrest reports or reports for summons; he believed in summary justice, 'a clip round the ear hole', 'a kick up the backside'. Anything contentious he would pass on to the probationary constable, ie me, to sort out. If it meant a court appearance or paperwork it would 'help my career development and give me experience'.

The sergeant had twenty-four-hour responsibility and lived at the police station. His day would be spread over the hours of eight am to midnight. Particularly on night duty, we would do pub visits, which meant the sergeant would normally imbibe a pint in every hostelry visited. At the end of the visits, Muggins would have to carry him back home and pour him on to his lounge floor, and expect grief from his better half the next day.

Communications in those days were non-existent for keeping in touch with the main police station at Morley. Hourly points had to be made at a telephone kiosk or at the police station in order that any calls for assistance could be passed on for attention. This also acted as a focal point for supervision by the sergeant or inspector who would visit you and check that appearance and pocket book were up to date. Bother followed if you were late, or did not cancel a point.

It was very embarrassing one night, having just purchased fish and chips, about to eat them in a shop doorway, when one saw the inspector's car approaching and had to conceal them in one's helmet. Not very comfortable, with grease flowing into your hair.

Transport was via foot, bus, or by 'noddy bike' when it was not broken down, very quiet, very slow, and very dangerous in winter. Many a time we have parted company on the ice. Places of interest that had to be visited for points were St Bernard's Mill, Gildersome, Briggs' Cafe,

The Police House

Cockersdale pub, the Railway pub, the brickworks and Drighlington crossroads.

Drig crossroads was a very important focal point to the local policeman, as four times a day it had to be visited to see local schoolchildren across the road. No matter what incident you were dealing with, this activity took priority. Drop tools and run.

A chief inspector in those days had an unusual 'fad', in that he believed every probationary constable should be proficient in traffic duty. To that end we would visit Drig crossroads, switch off the traffic lights and then he would display his wonderful array of traffic signals, with only him knowing what they were. That was OK until one day he waved two cars travelling in opposite directions into each other, then exited stage left, hence leaving the constable to sort out his mess and irate motorists.

There were three shifts that were regularly worked. Duties included:

Six am to two pm: self briefing, check all main street properties for signs of damage, burglary, school kids over road, deal with any overnight crime, general patrol duties.

Two pm to ten pm: road accidents, crime, kids causing nuisance, domestic disputes, under-age drinking.

Ten pm to six am: night's pub visits, property checks, dealing with drunks, contacting would-be burglars, vehicle checks.

Talking of burglars, there were some very intelligent ones in the area. For example, attended scene of burglary at plumbing company, entry to premises by broken window, and what does the ambitious copper find? A wallet and photograph of owner, plus name and address. Lives in house opposite young officer's. On visit to arrest would-be felon, he denies all knowledge, even though there is a clue in back garden, ie new copper piping and brass fittings sticking out under tarpaulin. He was nicked and prosecuted.

Another three likely lads decide to enter a local working men's club when it is snowing. After relieving the 'bandits' of their contents, they escape. They forget one important factor: footsteps in the snow, which are duly followed for a distance of four miles over fields and hedgerows by the determined young copper. They even try walking backwards to confuse. That's three more appearing before the 'beak'.

One of the favourite targets for burglars in those days was the Co-op stores, to steal cigs and booze. On one cold winter's night a taxi heading to

Bradford at three am was duly stopped, carrying the driver and a so-called fare. After giving a reasonable explanation they were allowed to proceed, only to be stopped again a mile up the road because it suddenly became apparent to the eagle-eyed copper that their coats on the back seat were spread out, but were level with the headrests of the front seats. On inspection, what was found? Booze and cigs. Where from? A local Co-op. Car boot full to brim. No Green Shield Stamps for those two late-night shoppers, but they did receive a 'bill' from Old Bill.

Drunks can be very annoying to a sober policeman, particularly at the weekend, when they are well oiled and we are working, the small men being the worst and most violent (having a point to prove, I suppose). One such character leaped up to try and 'head butt' the six-foot-two officer, bloodying his nose on the officer's torch, which was protruding from the front of his tunic. A local licensee rings at two am, saying his pub has been entered. He's about six foot four and twenty stone. Says he can hear voices and what sounds like 'snoring'. 'I'll wait upstairs 'til you arrive an' 'ave a good look round,' were his instructions. Yes, there was snoring and wheezing coming from downstairs, the culprits being the two bulldogs he owned. Another case solved; another embarrassed member of the public.

Another brave licensee rings to say a coach load of drunks are wrecking his pub and fighting in lumps, can you all come, quick! Yes, all two of us went quick, arrived, and saw what was going off, waited until they had knocked seven bells out of each other, and identified the two main instigators who were so drunk they fell against a rough wall, altering their facial appearance somewhat.

Working night duty entailed shaking hands with doorknobs, ie checking commercial properties for security. It's surprising what you find in some shop doorways, more embarrassing for him and her than me. On your way, please. One of the worst events with drunks was 'wazzing' in a shop doorway after leaving the pub. Not only does it smell, it runs into the shops and the unsuspecting copper gets his boots wet. Caught-in-the-act actions: give them a push so they get wet, make them wipe it up, with their clothing if necessary. A clout round the ear with a pair of leather gloves was instant justice, but not today: society has 'gone soft'.

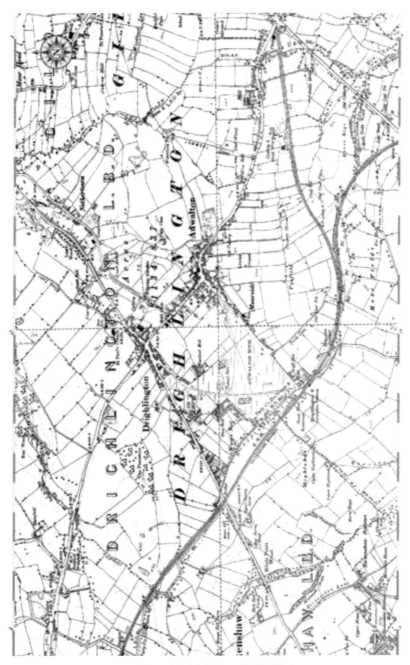

Map of Drighlington 1882–1892

An aerial view of Drighlington, circa 1930